The
Boston Driver's
HANDBOOK

The
Boston Driver's
HANDBOOK

The Almost Post Big Dig Edition

THIRD EDITION

Ira Gershkoff

and

Richard Trachtman

DA CAPO PRESS
A Member of the Perseus Books Group

Copyright © 2004 by Ira Gershkoff and Richard Trachtman

Maneuver illustrations by Pamela Cass Gershkoff. Photo on page 74 by Tom Moran. All other photos by Ira Gershkoff and Richard Trachtman.

Text Design by Jeff Williams
Set in 11 point Adobe Garamond by the Perseus Books Group

Cataloging-in-Publication data for this book is available from the Library of Congress.

First Da Capo Press edition 2004
ISBN 0–306–81326–2

Published by Da Capo Press
A Member of the Perseus Books Group
http://www.dacapopress.com

Da Capo Press books are available at special discounts for bulk purchases in the U.S. by corporations, institutions, and other organizations. For more informa-tion, please contact the Special Markets Department at the Perseus Books Group, 11 Cambridge Center, Cambridge, MA 02142, or call (800) 255-1514 or (617) 252-5298, or e-mail specialmarkets@perseusbooks.com.

1 2 3 4 5 6 7 8 9—07 06 05 04

Contents

1   **Getting Started**   **1**

The Philosophy of Boston Driving, 1
About Your Car, 3
License and Registration, 6
Inspection, 7
Insurance, 8
The Law—and How Little It Means, 9
Safety Considerations in Boston Driving, 10
Speaking the Language, 11
And Finally . . . , 12

2   **Street Layout**   **13**

Boston's City "Plan," 13
Major Neighborhoods, 16
Major Roads, 25

3   **The Big Dig: Boon or Boondoggle??**   **37**

The Big Dig Game Plan, 38
The Reality, 38
Dealing with the New Layout Downtown, 41
Other Words of Wisdom, 45

4   Basic Maneuvers   47

The Cutoff, 47
The Sidesqueeze, 49
Blocking, 50
Intersection Techniques, 51
Rotaries, 57
Weaving, 60
Beat the Guillotine, 60
Tailgating, 61
One-Way Streets, 62
U-Turns, 63
Bad Traffic Situations, 63

5   Common Obstacles   69

Pedestrians, 69
Trolleys and Buses, 72
Dogs, 73
Parked and Double-Parked Cars, 74
Bicycles, 76
Potholes, 79
Toll Booths, 82
Trucks, 84

6   Parking   87

Tickets, Tows, and Denver Boots, 87
Resident Stickers, 90
Is an Illegal Space Right for You? 91
Cruise Techniques, 93
Street Cleaning, 94
Where to Park, 95

7   Winter Driving   103

Snow Emergencies, 104
General Street Conditions, 105
Parking Space Entry and Exit Techniques, 106
Winter Maneuvers, 110

**8   Advanced Maneuvers and Harassment
      Techniques   113**

Why? 113
Taxicabs, 114
Cadillacs, 116
Honda Civics, 118
Advanced Turns, 120
Gas Station Turns, 124
Sidewalk Driving and Sidewalk Parking, 127
Deceptive Use of Signals, 129

9   The Future of Boston Driving   135

Final Exam   141

Getting Started

This book is about the world of Boston Driving, a fascinating sport currently practiced by more than three million licensed drivers in one of America's largest cities. You will find Boston Driving to be full of challenge and highly competitive. It's a dog-eat-dog situation: if you don't look out for Number One, at best you'll be left far, far behind. At worst you may be tempted to bury your car in a pothole and turn in your license. The sport has spread to other cities, but at this time no other city can come close to matching the caliber of Boston's own Boston Drivers.

The Philosophy of Boston Driving

There is perhaps only one place in North America where it is socially acceptable for human beings to give in to all of their primal urges while driving an automobile: Boston, Massachusetts. Whether it be a cleverly executed U-turn into a lonely parking space or just a routine left turn from the right lane of a busy street, the craft and artistry of a Boston Driver is a sight to behold, preferably at a safe distance. In Boston itself, one need only look to the nearest street corner to witness the crumbling of the stop sign barrier or perhaps hear the delicate crunch of a fender-bender. No one really seems to mind, least of all the Boston Police. In New England's largest city, Boston Drivers and their antics are inescapable.

In this book we will discuss the offensive driving skills you will need to know to ensure your survival as a motorist here. We will lead you step-by-step from basic techniques, such as the Cutoff and Sidesqueeze, through the more advanced maneuvers involving turns through gas stations or sidewalk driving. We will also cover the proper Boston handling of common hazards such as pedestrians, potholes, and cab drivers. For those who are not intimately familiar with the Boston area, we will cover the city's street design, focusing on the particular problems of getting around and parking in specific neighborhoods. And we'll even provide some pointers on how to cope with the nearly completed Big Dig—a massive highway project that has turned the entire metropolitan area into a construction battleground.

However, before we can go any further, we must set forth the First Commandment of Boston Driving:

COMMANDMENT 1

Thou shalt reach thy destination as quickly as possible. Everyone and everything else be damned.

Every lane change, maneuver, turn, acceleration, or deceleration is made with this ultimate goal in mind. Trivial socioeconomic considerations, such as gas mileage, wear and tear on the car, and especially safety, are to be ignored. Let's face it: "defensive driving" is an auto insurance company conspiracy and has no place in Boston Driving. The only things that count are arrival and survival.

Keep this goal in mind as you read this book. And remember, every driving maneuver is just a logical extension of the Boston

Driving philosophy. The most important car on the road is *your* car. *You* come first *always*. No special skills are required to become a first-rate Boston Driver; it is only necessary to have the proper attitude. If nothing else, keep that in mind, and you'll never go too far wrong.

Good luck!

About Your Car

A car is the most important piece of equipment you will need for Boston Driving. You should choose one carefully since your car will determine to some extent which maneuvers you can or cannot perform.

Small cars are preferable to large cars because they handle better and are more maneuverable. They are also much easier to park. On the other hand, big cars are better for hogging the road, if you are so inclined. Good acceleration and braking capabilities are assets for any car, big or small. You will often need them for cutting off other cars in heavy traffic.

It is always a good idea to have a few dents strategically placed around the car's body. The advantages are many. First, if you already have some dents, you won't worry about getting a few more. There is no surer way of getting involved in a fender-bender than worrying about getting involved in a fender-bender. Second, dents make your car a less attractive target for Boston's prolific car thieves. If they have a choice between your fully depreciated 1995 Civic and the brand new Porsche 911 Turbo parked next to you, guess who's going to get hit. Finally, when other drivers see your dents, they assume you have been in a number of accidents. They figure you are a lousy driver, maybe a little bit drunk and crazy as well. Your insurance was probably canceled long ago, they figure, so why should they risk life, limb, and property messing with you? Dents do wonders to clear the roadway around you.

It follows that a new car is the *worst* kind of car for Boston Driving. You will naturally worry about cracking it up, so you will. Other

The RIGHT kind of car for Boston Driving: 1965 Ford Falcon.

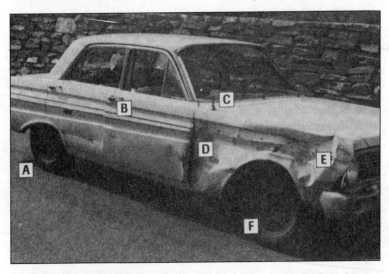

A. Semi-bald snow tires; B. Wire holding door closed; C. Coat hanger radio antenna; D. Liberal rust; E. Fender-bender dents; and F. Deluxe wheel covers.

drivers will take advantage of you unmercifully. Your car will be a prime target for theft. The new car condition is self-curing, however. Sooner or later your new car will receive its proper Boston baptism. After it has been stolen a few times and has caught a few nicks and scrapes banging up cars and pedestrians, it will no longer be new, and you won't have to worry about it anymore.

One other point on theft is worth mentioning. Boston is one of the nation's centers of excellence in car theft, but most likely the thief will be a fourteen-year-old boy who needs a car mainly to take him to the next car he will steal. Life being this way, you should make your car as unattractive as possible to the average fourteen-year-old. This means no titanium wheels, racing stripes, or Blaupunkt stereos, unless your car is wired to fry anyone who tampers with it. And please, absolutely nothing bigger than a nickel in plain sight.

The WRONG kind of car for Boston Driving: 2004 Toyota Celica.

After all, if you were a typical adolescent car thief, you wouldn't steal just any car; you'd want to exhibit a certain amount of taste. So you'd look for a car with lots of chrome and glitter and enough power to chase a 747, like a high-powered late model American sports car. You'd also want to sit in air-conditioned comfort (even in the winter) listening to your favorite CD on your victim's eardrum-shattering megabuck stereo system. From a theft standpoint, therefore, the ideal car to own is a beat-up American subcompact with at least 100,000 miles on it, a plain vanilla radio (no cassette or CD), semi-bald tires, and liberal rust on its body.

COMMANDMENT 2

Honor thy vehicle and keep it "holey."

License and Registration

A necessary step for becoming a card-carrying Boston Driver is to make a trip down to the Registry of Motor Vehicles. Grab a parking space anywhere in the vicinity. Then go inside, take a number, and wait. And wait. And wait some more. On a recent Friday afternoon, one prospective registrant was heard asking whether the numbers were being called in ascending or descending order. In view of the unpredictable and frequently unbearable wait, it is advisable to bring along extra food and water for this long siege. (You might also bring along this book so you can read up on what to do when you finally do get out, to make up for lost time.)

When at last you do arrive at the front of the line, you will then realize that you are in the midst of a Frustration Emporium. Registry employees are trained to tell you that you are in the wrong line. Once you are over that hurdle, they will say that you forgot something crucial, like your final report card from third grade.

Come in, take a number, sit down, and shut up.

When you finally leave the Registry sadder and poorer, holding the standard reform-school picture on your license, you will know that you have obtained the proper Boston driving credentials.

Lately the Registry has started to encourage people to mail in the paperwork to renew their automobile registrations. If you follow this procedure, you not only avoid the lines but also save a little money on the fee. Although we are certain that the postal process is some sort of trap—it's just too good to be true—we recommend that Boston Drivers take the risk and use it. After all, you will have to go back to the Registry soon enough when you buy a new car or renew your driver's license.

Inspection

Before you can legally launch your heap into the streets of Boston, you are supposed to have it inspected, as shown by a sticker on your windshield. Inspections used to be required by a specific date, which could be any time during the month. Since 2000, however, all inspection stickers expire on the last day of the month, creating huge lines on the last few days of every month. According to the Registry, the change was made in an effort to increase "customer convenience."

Nearly every garage in the state seems to be an inspection station. Look for a sign reproducing the current month's sticker, with the number large enough to be spotted by satellite. Generally, the attendant will eyeball your car, kick the tires, and ask you to test the signals. Then he or she will pull out a very long pole attached to a very expensive computer and stick it up your car's exhaust pipe. This is the emissions test, required because of the deteriorating quality of air in the entire industrial world, which has been traced to old gas-guzzlers in Boston. If you drive one of these relics, passing the emissions test is simple: drive to the inspection station first thing in the morning before the engine really warms up.

If the garage attendant actually starts to fiddle under the hood or mentions replaceable parts of your automobile, it is time to become very friendly and make some distracting conversation. In spring, ask whether Pedro Martinez will stay healthy enough to have another 20-win season. In the fall, discuss whether the Patriots can possibly repeat the miracle of Super Bowl XXXVI. If all else fails, greasing a palm with an extra couple of bucks should bring you the inspection sticker you need.

Insurance

Massachusetts has been long famous for having one of the highest auto insurance rates in the nation. There is good reason for this. Massachusetts has the most poorly maintained roads (see Chapter V, "Potholes"), the most inconsistent traffic law enforcement, the most skillful car thieves, and the highest number of accidents per capita of any state (i.e., the worst drivers). If these conditions continue to hold—and there is every reason to expect them to do so—there will be no relief in sight. Let's face it: driving in Massachusetts, especially Boston, is like driving the bumper cars at an amusement park (also known as "dodgems"). You don't have to pay attention to the condition of your already beat-up car; try not to get hit, but don't worry if you are.

Auto insurance is supposed to spread the cost of accidents over all motorists, but it frequently doesn't quite work out that way. Massachusetts requires minimum coverage per accident of $20,000 for injury to one person, $40,000 for all bodily injuries, and $5,000 for property loss. But everyone knows that at current levels of auto repair costs, lawyers' fees, and especially medical expenses, $20,000/$40,000/$5,000 won't buy a Band-Aid.

It is the same story with collision insurance, although collision is not legally required. Collision insurance is designed to protect against loss in the value of your car due to an accident, but most cars still alive after three years on the streets of Boston have nothing left worth insuring for collision anyway. In many cases, collision insurance will cost more than 100 percent of the book value of the car, a guaranteed losing proposition.

Over the years, the Massachusetts state legislature has originated many innovative approaches to the auto insurance problem. State Representative Michael Dukakis was among those who led the legislature in passing the nation's first "no-fault" auto insurance law in the early 1970s. All auto accidents with less than $2,000 in property damage or bodily injury claims were to be settled for each involved driver by his or her own insurance company. For a year or two, the system worked beautifully.

But Massachusetts drivers eventually turned out to be much more innovative than the laws that regulate them. One hundred dollars' worth of bent fender tended to show up as $600 worth of body work on the estimate, and the motorist would pocket the difference. Mysterious back injuries would appear, almost always costing between $1,950 and $1,999, and then be miraculously cured. Some accident "victims" would manufacture enough medical expenses and lost work time to push the total claim over $2,000 and cut in the lawyers, something that the no-fault law was designed to avoid in the first place.

Of course, the insurance buyers pay for all this scamming, but in general, Boston Drivers are not very concerned by it. For one thing, there is a point system that rewards safe, experienced drivers—and drivers who don't get caught. The state attorney general can be counted on to keep insurance rates down when they rise to outrageous heights or when an election approaches. And apparently some Boston Drivers just bide their time, waiting for that perfect opportunity to find a new and innovative way to beat the system.

The Law—and How Little It Means

An authentic, bonafide moving violation used to be a real collector's item among Boston Drivers. Once upon a time, an acquaintance of ours drove the wrong way down Boylston Street from the Public Garden all the way to the Prudential Center before being stopped by the police. They informed him that the "preferred direction" was the other way and sent him along.

But times have changed, and with the change has come a much more vigorous enforcement of the traffic laws—sort of. Certainly more moving violation tickets are being given out. But it's important to bear in mind that the reason for the stepped-up enforcement has very little to do with promoting traffic safety and quite a lot to do with ballooning budget deficits at the local and state levels. This presents a challenge to all card-carrying Boston Drivers, who must now cope with a rejuvenated traffic court system whose primary goal is to raise money.

For instance, a highway speeding ticket costs $100 for the first 10 m.p.h. over the speed limit, including a $50 surcharge for a head injury trust fund, and each additional m.p.h. over that adds another $10. Catching someone driving 90 m.p.h. on Route 128, therefore, earns the state a speedy $350. Some civic-minded motorists have contributed $500 or more under this system.

This is not to say that there has been a notable decrease in the use of Boston Driving techniques. Far from it! In fact, speeding, going the wrong way down a one-way street, illegal turns, and all those other violations that fill the law books are just as much a part of the Boston Driver's repertoire as ever. The difference is that there is a renewed emphasis on *form*. You must avoid the *appearance* of impropriety. For example, illegal turns should be done smoothly, without signaling and without guilt. One-way maneuvers should be done in reverse gear—your car will be facing the right way, you won't stand out, and you won't get a ticket. Establish your rule of the road with finesse and class, so that it appears to be the natural order of things.

If you should get a moving violation (even the best Boston Drivers have off-days), keep in mind that even the priciest traffic ticket is tiny compared to your insurance bill. Just write it off as a cost of participating in the sport of Boston Driving.

Safety Considerations in Boston Driving

None.

Speaking the Language

The newcomer to Boston is always impressed by the dialect spoken here. Westerners think they are in a foreign country; Midwesterners are tolerant; Southerners fall in love with it; Washingtonians turn up their noses; and New Yorkers and Philadelphians laugh out loud when they hear it. Yes, indeed, it really is English that Bostonians speak, but you have to keep your ears wide open and remember a few translation rules.

Pronunciation may best be characterized as lazy. Bostonians don't like to finish off their words; speech is somewhat slurred as one word rolls awkwardly into the next. Properly done, Bostonese is louder and coarser than normal English. The biggest problem for the novice is the pathetic pronunciation of the letter *R*, especially at the end of a word or syllable. For example:

AR is pronounced "ah" (*pahk* the *cah*)
ER is pronounced "uh" (what a muht*huh*)
OR is pronounced "aw" (give it m*aw* gas)
ERS is pronounced "iz" (watch those Boston dri*viz*)

To give you an idea of what to expect, we turn to noted citizen and part-time MBTA bus driver Harry ("High-Gear") Harrison, for a testimonial on the relative advantages of the Massachusetts Turnpike over alternate roads:

The Pike shuah is fast, but geez, it is expensive. Ya get on by the rivvuh theyuh, ya know, neah Cambridge, and take it out to route one-twunny-eight, and it'll costya two dol-luhs. And at rush houah, especially on Frideez, the cahs sometimes back up clear to Hahvuhd Squeyuh. I guess ya hafta take it if yaw headed faw New Yawk uh Hahtfuhd aw sump'm, but if yaw goin to Concuhd aw nawth to New Hampshuh aw some place like that, I'm shuah ya could find a bettuh way.

And Finally . . .

You now should have all the necessary hardware to learn how to become a full-fledged Boston Driver. You have a car, license, registration, inspection sticker, and insurance. You also know how to communicate with the natives. Add a little common sense, and you would have enough to drive anywhere—anywhere except Boston, that is. Only after you read the rest of this book can you claim to have the proper qualifications to reach your destination in minimum time and to truly enjoy the sport of Boston Driving.

2

Street Layout

With its deepwater harbor and access to two navigable rivers (Charles and Mystic), Boston was a natural spot to build a city back in the seventeenth century, when those things mattered. Surrounded on three sides by water, the city's limited access to the mainland made it relatively easy to defend against Indians, French, or other hostile forces.

One is not likely to find the layout of the streets of Greater Boston quite so natural, however. The hodgepodge of one- and two-way streets pointing in different directions, curving wildly, merging from three lanes to one and back again, and sprinkled with "No Left Turn" signs, is enough to unsettle any anarchist. In this chapter we will attempt to unravel the mystery somewhat by presenting a few useful pointers in getting around the city.

Boston's City "Plan"

The most widely accepted theory on the nonsense of Boston street layout is known as the Cow Pasture Theory. To understand it, one must again return to seventeenth-century Boston. In those days, residents liked to graze their cows on the Common and do a little socializing at the same time. On the often roundabout way to and from their barns, the cows would make paths. The biggest of these

In today's metropolitan area, Paul Revere would
never have made it all the way to Concord.

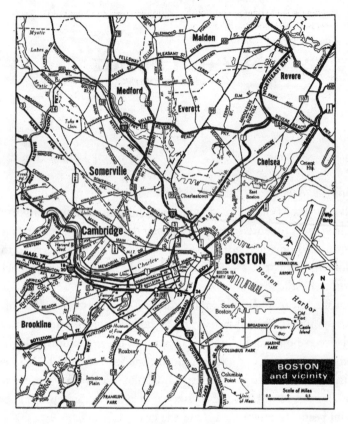

became Beacon Street; Tremont, Washington, and all the rest followed. The reason Boston's streets are what they are today, so the
theory goes, is that they were designed by cows, and the cows were
simply not clever enough to envision the coming of the automobile
250 years later when deciding where to make their tracks.

This theory also explains the development of all the squares and
circles in the city. With so many cow paths intersecting at a variety
of angles, squares and circles naturally developed. Many were used
as meeting places for the Pilgrims long before the days of Paul

Revere, New England clam chowder, and the Boston Red Sox. However they came about, there is no rhyme or reason to the location, frequency, or density of squares. To this day, Boston remains a place where the unsuspecting motorist can drive in circles for hours while trying to go between squares.

Another less popular rumor has it that the city planner back in those days had a soft spot for Italian food, and he saw the street plan one day in his bowl of spaghetti. While this theory does not have the following of the Cow Pasture Theory, it nevertheless could well explain the random development of the street layout. Looking at a map of Boston, one can see the great appeal of this explanation.

The point of this discussion is that there is no substitute in Boston Driving for a thorough knowledge of the roads. Knowing which lane to drive in or where to turn in certain situations is a key factor in executing many maneuvers. Also good to know are shortcuts through residential areas, pothole locations, and traffic light cycles.

If you are in an unfamiliar part of town, don't even try to navigate by street signs. Most intersections don't have them; those that do are likely to be turned. Major streets are almost never marked, on the theory that if you don't know where you are, you don't belong there. Cross streets might be, but the information seldom will do you any good. It is assumed that motorists always know which street they are driving on. But since even experienced Boston Drivers do not always know where they are, and since there is no logic to the layout of the streets, getting lost is a common occurrence.

COMMANDMENT 3

Thou shalt ever resist the temptation to put thy trust in street signs.

Major Neighborhoods

Downtown

The downtown area consists of most of the land between the Boston Common and the Central Artery. It includes Government Center, the financial district, Downtown Crossing and other shopping areas, the old Combat Zone, and Chinatown. It is one of the oldest sections of the city. Streets are usually narrow and almost always one-way, and pedestrians outnumber cars at least twenty to one. Don't worry if you get lost: because of the cow pasture layout, you'll end up back where you started before you know it. It is the most congested part of the city, and there just isn't much room for cars. Traffic is terrible all the time, and the pedestrians will harass you to boot. We don't recommend driving in this part of town unless absolutely necessary.

Back Bay

In the mid-1800s, Boston embarked on a number of land reclamation projects. The largest of these is now known as Back Bay, so called because it was originally a shallow marsh that would flood at high tide. The mouth of the Charles River was then in the vicinity of the current B.U. Bridge. Because of its relative youth, most of the original townhouses built on the reclaimed land are still standing and in use.

Furthermore, Back Bay shocks us with its parallel streets intersecting at right angles. To add still more sanity, the streets are in alphabetical order. Any seasoned Boston Driver can rattle them off for you: Arlington, Berkeley, Clarendon, Dartmouth, Exeter, Fairfield, Gloucester, and Hereford. Most people don't know that the naming pattern continues beyond Massachusetts Avenue: Ipswich, Jersey, and Kilmarnock.

The street closest to the Charles River is called Back Street, aptly named because it faces the rear of the even-numbered houses on Beacon Street. Drivers sometimes take Back Street to avoid the traffic on Beacon or Marlborough Streets. However, it is used mainly for parking, garbage pickup (and occasionally dumping), and committing violent crimes. Garbage scavengers, car thieves, muggers, and murderers flourish in this isolated environment. Incredibly, Back Street is two-way, and it is often difficult for two cars to get by each other. Further complicating life for those seeking speedy passage through Back Bay on Back Street are frequent patches of rough pavement and the speed bumps that have been placed in their path. These obstacles have little effect on the tow trucks that are the mainstay of Back Street's economy. They always have plenty to do, for there is no public parking permitted on Back Street.

Beacon Hill

Another part of Boston that dates to colonial times is Beacon Hill. It is roughly the area enclosed by Charles, Beacon, and Cambridge Streets. This neighborhood is characterized by small, expensive townhouses and narrow, hilly streets. Because of the nostalgic

Back Street

atmosphere and the proximity to downtown Boston, Beacon Hill is an "in" place to live.

Driving through Beacon Hill is another matter, however. It can be difficult to maneuver through this area because of the narrow one-way streets, many of which are on especially steep inclines as well. To make things even worse, the "preferred" direction of certain streets has been known to have been suddenly reversed on occasion.

The electric lights on some streets can easily be mistaken for gas lamps, and a few streets are cobblestoned to this day. On some street corners, lit red globes indicate the presence of a fire alarm. We know of one poor soul who encountered one of these red globes one night when he had had a few too many. Thinking he was in the presence of a red traffic light, our hero patiently waited for it to turn green. For all we know, he is still waiting.

The North End

The North End is an old, predominantly Italian part of town. (This is where "Wednesday is Prince Spaghetti Day" came from.) Like Beacon Hill, streets are narrow and occasionally cobblestoned. In addition, the many fine restaurants of the area bring on a high incidence of double-parking. Because of the combination of double-parking and narrow streets, don't be surprised to find that the street you are on is unnavigable.

Street fairs have also been known to play havoc with Boston Drivers navigating around the North End, particularly during the summer. Many a motorist has embarked on a carefully planned route to a North End destination, only to discover the way blocked by a block party honoring this week's patron saint. Often the driver will stop the car, be invited to join the party, and never be heard from again. The alert Boston Driver must therefore carefully gauge the life-threatening risks of driving into the North End on a summer weekend.

Residents of the North End are fiercely loyal, pro-union Americans, and foreign cars are treated accordingly. Unfamiliar cars

Almost all street parking in the North
End is reserved for residents . . .

. . . and whatever's left over is set aside
for street festivals.

have been known to be given the same type of North End "visitor's welcome." Standard procedure for the North End "enforcers" is to break into a car, swipe whatever personal property is found (including, but not limited to, cannolis), sort through it, and arrange for any unwanted merchandise to be hauled away along with the dismantled sections of the old Central Artery. So, if you have to bring a high-risk car into the North End, make sure you have kept up with your protection payments.

Waterfront

The waterfront area runs along Atlantic Avenue between the North End and South Station. For the last several years it has been the most rapidly developing area of Boston; luxury high-rise apartments now stand where dilapidated warehouses used to be. Skyscraper hotels and office buildings stand side by side, obliterating all memory of the old neighborhood and its views of the water. In one way the waterfront has changed little, however: its street layout. The curving lattice of one-ways like Milk and India brings to mind the peaceful images of wandering cows.

The revitalized Faneuil Hall Marketplace, which borders the waterfront area, has been immensely popular among residents and tourists alike. These tourists (and their cars) are the primary source of trouble for the waterfront Boston Drivers. You can spot them easily by their out-of-state plates, their unusually fresh-looking cars (provided this is their first day in town), and the bewildered look on their faces as they struggle to make sense of the street layout of Boston. Because of their lack of knowledge on the rules of the road for Boston Drivers, they can be very erratic and unpredictable.

For the same reason, however, you will find tourists easy to take advantage of. For some reason they have a lot of trouble navigating along the frequent curves on Atlantic Avenue. Apparently they are worried that one false move will send them over the edge of the nearest wharf into the murky waters of Boston Harbor. They also seem to be intimidated by the presence of the Big Dig construction. It just could be that they've abandoned all hope, as the frequent construction-related shifts in the direction of traffic flow have rendered the Mapquest printouts they brought from home totally useless. (With few Boston street names marked with signs, computerized directions aren't worth very much anyway.)

As of this writing, you would need an artist's rendering to get an idea of what the post–Big Dig waterfront will look like. For the first time since Ted Williams patrolled Fenway's Green Monster, the eyesore that has been the elevated Central Artery will be gone. This will enable Boston's historic waterfront to reconnect to downtown. Will visitors returning to Boston for the first time even recognize this new waterfront as they drive out of the Sumner Tunnel? Or will they wonder whether they've landed in the wrong city? We're confident that, after a few minutes of helplessly trying to navigate the narrow criss-crossing one-way streets that make up the downtown grid, anyone with even a little Boston driving experience will realize they could be nowhere else.

Allston/Brighton

Although the physical layout of the streets of Allston/Brighton is not particularly threatening, this area boasts the most aggressive, arrogant and selfish drivers in the Boston Area. Here are the cream of the crop: the most Boston of Boston Drivers.

Out-of-state plates are common in Allston/Brighton, as the area has a pedominantly student population. Many residents are young and transient; most of their cars are old and veterans of many a fender-bender. New cars are seldom seen since few residents are rich enough to afford a full-time bodyguard for their car, and without one, a new car becomes indistinguishable from the masses within a week.

Commonwealth Avenue in Allston/Brighton is unique among the streets of Boston in that it has six lanes of traffic, two lanes of trolley tracks, and three medians. Two of the lanes are given to a serv-

Brighton Intersection Dynamics

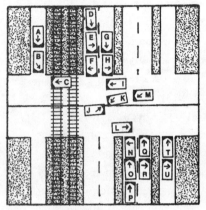

The light has just turned yellow on Harvard Street (left to right). C and I are proceeding through the intersection on Harvard St. toward Allston. L is going the opposite way, toward Brookline. M and K are trying to turn left onto Commonwealth Avenue outbound; J is trying to turn inbound. All other drivers are waiting for the Comm. Ave. light to turn green. E is trying a left turn from the right lane: difficult, but by no means unusual. Relatively speaking, the situation is quite calm.

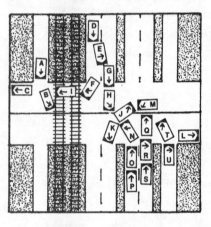

The action begins to pick up, as B enters the intersection for a left turn. C escapes to Allston. D waits as E changes lanes for left turn. F begins right turn but must stop, as I is cut off by B. G follows H, who must go around J, who is waiting to take a left. K takes a left and is on the way toward Brighton; L proceeds to Brookline. M must wait for J; N for K; O and P must wait for N; and R and S must wait for T, who is trying to get on the main part of Comm. Ave. from Parking Lot Row. T yields to Q, who is waiting for M to take a left, and U will wait for T, then follow L.

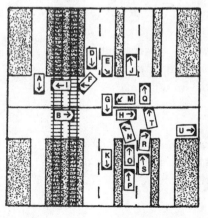

Congestion reaches a peak, as B sees enough daylight to take a left, allowing A into the intersection just in time to cut off I. F begins a right turn behind I, but does not get far enough for D to proceed. E and M are blocked by G, who in turn is cut off by N continuing a left turn in the wrong lane. H must wait for T, who is following Q. O and P are still waiting for N to get out of the way, and R and S are waiting for T. J, K, Q, and U have clear sailing.

Brighton Intersection Dynamics *(continued)*

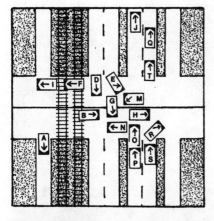

Action finally begins to subside. A crosses intersection, allowing I and F a clear road to Allston. B continues toward Brookline, but is cut off by G, who is still waiting for N. N must continue in the wrong lane around B. D is stymied when reaching B. E, frustrated by now, begins a turn by going in the wrong lane around M the way N is going around B. M is still waiting for G. H could go, but R made a wide turn and cut H off. O, P, and S are still waiting for the intersection to clear. J, Q, and T travel on unimpeded.

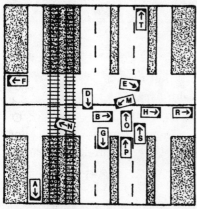

N continues in the wrong lane, allowing G to break into the clear. This allows B to move forward a few feet and lets D move on. E continues in the wrong lane, planning to move in behind H and R. Poor M continues to wait for a break and holds up O, P, and S. A, F, and T leave the scene.

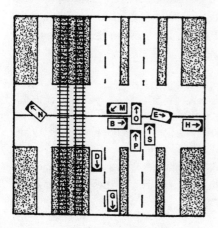

The intersection is nearly clear when the Commonwealth Avenue light turns yellow. B must wait for O and P to cross the intersection. When B goes by, M can finish the left turn. (Note that M sat in the intersection for the entire light cycle. Had M been as good a Boston Driver as N, this never would have happened.) N and E are making their way back to the right side of the street. Everyone else has an unobstructed path.

A former new car from Allston/Brighton

ice road otherwise known as "Parking Lot Row." It is unclear for what use these lanes were intended, but they do provide the only on-street parking for Commonwealth Avenue.

They extend about three miles from Brighton Avenue all the way to Chestnut Hill Avenue. The only reason to travel in these roads is if you want to park. If you try to travel in these lanes, you will be hung up by drivers pulling in and out of spaces, looking for spaces, double-parking, or talking to their friends. In the winter these roads are never plowed, so you might end up getting stuck or at least have to help push someone out of a drift. At cross streets it is often difficult to turn from Parking Lot Row to the main part of Commonwealth Avenue, and a left turn is a real challenge.

Cambridge

Seat of two of the world's foremost universities, Cambridge is not very enlightened on the subject of street layout. The Cow Pasture Theory holds up very well here, as Harvard, Central Tech, Kendall, Porter, Inman, and Lechmere Squares testify. All these squares have numerous streets coming together at the intersection, resulting in frequent traffic bottlenecks. Cambridge was the inspiration for the "one way the wrong way" maneuver (see Chapter IV, One-Way Streets"). This was born out of necessity; with the long, narrow one-way streets, it would be too much to expect anyone to take the trouble to go around.

A discussion of street layout in Cambridge must center around Massachusetts Avenue, the principal thoroughfare and lifeblood of this city. Seldom less than four lanes wide, it passes through nearly all of the commercial areas of the city and is within walking distance of almost every resident.

Traffic along parts of Mass. Ave. can be incredibly dense and move unbelievably slowly. A relentless string of traffic lights will dot your path, and pedestrians can usually move faster than cars. Whenever possible, keep to the middle of Mass. Ave. Too far right will find you waiting for buses, double-parked cars, and people looking for parking. Too far left, and you will be behind cars attempting left turns. If there are only two lanes, stay alert and play it by ear.

Of late Cambridge has taken on a suburban air, meaning there are many more malls. The glitzy CambridgeSide Galleria, one block from the Charles River, rivals the established malls along Route 128. It also has a large underground parking Garage—too large, in fact. There are more parking spaces than the city's permit allowed. Therefore, while in this little corner of Cambridge parking has become cheap and almost easy, the city has restricted spaces elsewhere (see Chapter VI, "Resident Stickers").

Major Roads

Central Artery/Southeast Expressway

All eyes will be on Interstate 93 when the Big Dig is finally done (supposedly in 2005). With the opening of the underground

Southeast Expressway Northbound

Central Artery, I-93 should become the crown jewel of the interstate highway system. The Southeast Expressway, long considered the grandmother of all Boston highways, is the portion of I-93 that extends from the southern end of the artery in downtown southward to Route 3 in Braintree. North of downtown, I-93 crosses the Charles River on the Leonard P. Zakim Bunker Hill Bridge and continues northwesterly through New Hampshire and finally into Vermont where it ends.

The new Central Artery, with far fewer exits than its predecessor, is designed to be a through route. The good news is that this may relieve some of the previous congestion due to drivers traveling from one local destination to another switching to alternative routes. The bad news is that it can be expected to attract long-distance drivers who had previously bypassed downtown Boston on Interstates 95 and 495. So don't count on zipping through downtown, except maybe at 3 A.M.

The prediction here is that the Southeast Expressway will continue to be the route that people use more than any other to come in and out of Boston. The Big Dig project, for all its glory, will not improve the Expressway for most of its length. Numerous large, slow-moving trucks will continue to contribute their foul exhaust to this already overcrowded and overpolluted highway. This is one road where getting a speeding ticket during rush hour is virtually impossible because the posted speed limit of 55 m.p.h. can rarely, if ever, be attained. Traffic congestion on I-93 is as much of a Boston tradition as the bean and the cod. (We cover the ramifications of the new underground Central Artery in Chapter III, "The Big Dig: Boon or Boondoggle??". Stay tuned.)

Storrow Drive

Running south and west from Leverett Circle along the Charles River, Storrow Drive is a major cross-town expressway. This road is appreciated by Boston Drivers for its quick access to downtown locations. But the road is not without its faults. Potholes and sunken manholes are such fixtures that many Boston Drivers know them by name. Because of the importance of Storrow Drive as a commuter

Final stretch of Storrow Drive chaos

Famous Storrow Drive landmark customized for the baseball playoffs

road, there is little likelihood they will ever be fixed. Even if they were, the relentless battering of rubber on road would ensure permanent scars in the pavement.

Out-of-state drivers who have the misfortune of attempting Storrow Drive inevitably have trouble with the placement of exit and entrance ramps. For example, the entrance from Beacon Street to Storrow Drive deposits the motorist onto the fast lane with little visibility of traffic coming from the other side of the overpass. In addition, numerous left exits with little or no warning on the outbound side require a thorough knowledge of the layout of Storrow Drive before it can be effectively utilized by the Boston Driver. Stay in the middle lane if you are heading to the suburbs.

Another hazard, usually occurring only in summer, is a concert on the Esplanade. At these times Storrow Drive is likely to become a parking lot. Boston Drivers seem to have no qualms whatsoever about parking their cars in the outbound lanes of Storrow Drive. Free rock concerts and fireworks displays have been known to attract upwards of 200,000 people, many of whom take advantage of the free parking on Storrow Drive.

The newcomer to Boston Driving might be intrigued by the numerous signs on Storrow Drive that give the road-clearance height. In spite of all the signs, a truck will periodically get wedged under a bridge because the driver could not believe the clearance was too low. If not for the fact that traffic then backs up for several miles behind the accident, it would probably be an amusing sight. On one morning some years back, a truck carrying a load of industrial-strength scissors became stuck under a bridge in this manner. As a result, some of the cargo spilled onto the pavement. Over thirty cars got flat tires, and two of these got four flat tires. The back-up lasted well into the afternoon.

Harbor Tunnels

Two places where there is never a shortage of carbon monoxide are the Sumner and Callahan Tunnels. (The shiny new Ted Williams Tunnel has some catching up to do, but give it a few decades and it will proudly take its place alongside its predecessors.) The tunnels provide a direct link between downtown Boston and Logan Airport.

The Callahan Tunnel: the gates of hell

They also provide the only link to East Boston, but nobody cares about that except the people of East Boston, Winthrop, and Revere.

Even on the best of days, a trip through either of these tunnels will quickly wipe the smile off your face. Two crowded, narrow lanes in each direction assure that your trip under Boston Harbor will be lengthy and unpleasant. Worst of all, the vintage tunnels smell like a three-week-old bologna sandwich. Open your car window at your own risk.

On top of all this, you have to pay for the privilege: a $3.00 toll is levied on each inbound trip. There is no toll for cars leaving downtown Boston, presumably as a reward to Boston Drivers who have wisely elected to leave town while their automobiles are still running. Traffic is almost always backed up at the booths; typical delays range from five minutes at lunch time to fifty minutes at rush hour. (Proper toll booth techniques are discussed in Chapter V, "Toll Booths.") Arriving travelers at Logan Airport are in for a surprise when they find out that even though they are only three miles from downtown Boston, it will take them an hour and a half to get there.

In conclusion, you really haven't made it as a Boston Driver until you can claim to have run out of gas in the middle of the Sumner or Callahan Tunnel and emerged with both your life and your car intact.

COMMANDMENT 4

Lead thyself not through the shadow
of the Callahan Tunnel if thou art
low on fuel.

Tobin Bridge

Also known as the Mystic River Bridge, the Tobin carries tens of thousands of commuters daily from the North Shore across the Mystic River into Boston. Judging from the traffic flow during rush hour, most of these commuters could go faster if they walked. The design of the bridge is unique in that the inbound lanes are directly above the outbound lanes. On a clear day, the view of the city from the upper deck (inbound lanes) can be quite spectacular.

Because traffic across it is so heavy, the bridge is always in need of repair. Because it is constantly being repaired, traffic on the bridge is always heavy. The concrete lane dividers are periodically rearranged, providing a continual challenge of proper lane positioning. Toll booth attendants on the Tobin's inbound level extort a $2.00 toll to cover the round trip. As with the tunnels, drivers entering Boston in essence pay for their trip out of town before their arrival. Though it may be tempting to seek a toll-free route into Boston from the north, you will most likely find yourself driving far enough to enter the city from the west, and spending as much on gasoline as you would have spent at the toll booth.

Another use of tolls is to buy paint for the bridge. One reliable way for out-of-staters to identify the Tobin Bridge is that it is constantly being repainted. A series of yellow lights shining against the sickly green supports of the bridge unfortunately appears in any

The Tobin Temple

nighttime panorama of the city of Boston. Former Boston mayor Maurice G. Tobin probably couldn't have dreamed what a pain in the neck his legacy has become.

Mass. Pike

By far the fastest land route across the state is the Massachusetts Turnpike, usually referred to as the "Mass. Pike." The Pike forms the easternmost leg of Interstate 90, a vital transcontinental route that extends all the way to Seattle. The Pike is the straightest and fastest way out of Boston, but in recent years it has been frequently clogged with traffic during rush hours. The Big Dig construction has now extended the Pike eastward 3.5 miles under South Boston and on to Logan Airport and East Boston via the Ted Williams Tunnel.

The main problem with the Pike is that it is a rich man's road. To travel the nine miles of the Extension (from Weston to South

Subliminal message on the Mass. Pike

Station) costs $2.00. That's over twenty cents per mile, thereby making the Mass. Pike Extension one of the most expensive toll roads in the United States. For this reason alternate routes are frequently used, but none of these can match the speed and convenience of the Mass. Pike. Aside from the price tag, the Pike suffers from an additional hazard: an occasional long home run from Fenway Park has been known to come to rest on its inbound lanes.

Route 128/I-95

This road is the major bypass around Boston, connecting the North Shore communities with those on the west side of town and the South Shore. Route 128 is Boston's Beltway: if not for the Atlantic Ocean, it would completely encircle the city, never getting closer than about ten miles.

The part of 128 between Norwood and Peabody has also been designated as Interstate 95 since the mid-1990s. However, most Boston Drivers still refer to it as "128." While the Federal Highway Administration would like the I-95 designation to stick, everyone knows that the Massachusetts high-tech industries grew up on 128, not 95. For several decades to come, any reference to this road as "95" will immediately brand you as a tourist and subject you to contempt and ridicule from your fellow Boston Drivers.

Both Route 128 and the Southeast Expressway I-93 are heavily traveled commuter roads, but here the similarity ends. The Southeast Expressway goes through the heart of the city; 128 goes through the heart of the suburbs. The S.E. Expressway has historically been loaded with potholes; 128 is normally well-maintained. Traffic backs up everywhere on the S.E. Expressway; only at a few predictable places on 128. While drivers on the Southeast Expressway seldom go over the speed limit, drivers on 128 seldom go under it.

One final note of caution: Beware of the extremely short entrance and exit lanes on 128 up north in Peabody and Danvers.

Which way is up??

Apparently, these were designed under the assumption that every car has turbocharged acceleration and brakes. Before taking on this stretch of highway, make sure you and your passengers are strapped in and up for a roller-coaster ride.

Jamaicaway

While traveling this road, don't ever try to pass anything bigger than a motorcycle. Narrow lanes and sharp curves banked the wrong way make the Jamaicaway a Fools' Paradise for Boston Drivers. Although it is four lanes wide, the roller coaster design makes it impossible to ride two abreast; those who try are given the choice between a head-on collision or a sideswipe. It is even more effective at catching drunken drivers than the State Police: many a drunk has grown weary of following this poorly lit concrete death trap and has found him- or herself sitting in four feet of dirty water in Jamaica Pond.

Route 1

U.S. 1 goes both north and south of Boston. It is the same Route 1 that extends from northern Maine to the Florida Keys. Formerly the only north–south road through town, it is still one of the most important. Route 1 north of Boston is known for its never-ending supply of gas stations, "no-tell" motels, shopping centers, and junk food restaurants. If you are stranded on Route 1, rest assured that you are never more than a two-minute walk from a gas station or a five-minute walk from a restaurant.

Route 93

This is the major road to New Hampshire and Quebec Province. In downtown Boston, I-93 is the Central Artery, with all of its traffic-related obstacles to Boston Driving. North of the city, I-93 is a typical interstate highway: secure and spacious, and therefore boring. Traffic seldom backs up except in the vicinity of the Charles River crossing, where a painful experience can be expected any hour of day or night. (Route 93 also includes the Southeast Expressway, but as far as we are concerned, they are two different concepts.)

The most striking visual element of I-93 is the new Leonard P. Zakim Bunker Hill Bridge, which spans the Charles River connecting Boston and Charlestown. The Bridge has a unique cable wire construction that looks like an overgrown harp. Its design included numerous holes in the structure specifically to allow sunlight to filter to the river below, which is necessary to enable the alewife fish to spawn. (How any fish could survive in the Charles River, much less spawn, is a mystery to us.) Nevertheless, it is certain to become a dramatic new icon for the post–Big Dig Boston skyline, as well as a modern complement to the nearby Bunker Hill Monument. Modern rush-hour traffic will make the Zakim Bridge the site of the re-enactment of the Battle of Bunker Hill every weekday morning and afternoon for the foreseeable future.

Route 2

This road traverses the entire length of Massachusetts, beginning at the Charles Street side of the Boston Common and extending to the New York State border. But most Boston Drivers think of Route 2 as the eight-mile stretch of high-speed divided highway between North Cambridge, near Fresh Pond, and Route 128. Except for the inevitable back-up on the eastbound side during morning rush hour, Route 2 is as fast as you like it, and some like it pretty fast. But beware of those gung-ho out-of-state drivers who come barreling down the big hill on the eastbound side and discover too late that Route 2 terminates quite abruptly in a traffic circle. This situation may be more than their brakes (or yours) can handle.

All good things have their price, and Route 2 is no exception. Starting from downtown, the inexperienced driver will never be able to navigate the five miles of winding, treacherous, and usually clogged roadway that separates him or her from the real beginning of Route 2. To get there, the motorist has basically three choices: (1) Storrow or Memorial Drive to Fresh Pond Parkway and follow the signs (f you can); (2) take I-93 north to Route 16, then take a coffee break in Medford Square before backtracking down Route 16 to Route 2; or (3) take the Mass. Pike and forget the whole thing.

3

The Big Dig:
Boon or Boondoggle??

The Big Dig is the latest of a long line of major public works projects in Boston. Since the first shovel of dirt was lifted from South Boston in December 1991, the Big Dig has sucked up more than $14 billion of public funds, disrupted traffic and commerce in the city, and left much of the city looking like a war zone. But the vision of putting the Central Artery underground was compelling and kept everyone in full support, especially since the Feds were picking up the lion's share of the tab.

Now there is light at the end of the tunnel, so to speak. The estimated date for the end of construction is 2005. By that time, the Central Artery (a.k.a. the Fitzgerald Expressway and I-93) will be underground with 4–5 lanes in each direction. The elevated Artery, which has been an eyesore for a half century, will be torn down, releasing twenty-five acres of prime city land for the Rose Kennedy Greenway, a planned public city park.

So does the completion of the Big Dig mean the beginning of a new millennium of traffic nirvana in Boston? We'll examine this question (and many others) in this chapter. For seasoned Boston Drivers, handling the aftermath of the Big Dig will be just as important as negotiating the reverse curve on Storrow Drive. It's an important skill that every Boston Driver needs to acquire.

The Big Dig Game Plan

In order to understand how to cope with the new Boston Driving situations brought on by the Big Dig, it is important to understand the historical perspective. Conceived in the early 1980s by a strange-bedfellow alliance between transportation planners and politicians, the Central Artery/Harbor Tunnel project, better known as the Big Dig, was seen as the solution to Boston's traffic problems. Its original scope included an underground Central Artery and a new harbor tunnel between South Boston and Logan Airport (a.k.a. the Ted Williams Tunnel). Capacity of the underground Artery would be 4–5 lanes in each direction instead of three.

The old (and ugly) Central Artery structure would then be dismantled, leaving land for a public park or some other noncommercial use. Total cost would be a paltry $2.5 billion. The city would be prettier, traffic would move faster, and everybody would be happier, right?

The Reality

Now that the end of the project is in sight, it is possible to tally a fairly accurate scorecard. When the digging began in 1991, the project's completion date was projected to be 2003. It will actually be more like 2005. Now that's not so bad—two years late out of twelve. No doubt many of our readers had high school term papers that were as late as that.

Cost is another matter. The original $2.5 billion estimate is now a vivid reality of nearly $15 billion, a 500 percent increase. Massachusetts Congressman Barney Frank questioned the wisdom of lowering the artery, observing that it would be cheaper to raise the city. There were certainly enough players sharing the pie that when technical problems later developed, it led to a feeding frenzy

The $15 Billion Tunnel

of contractors and experts of every size and stripe coming to the trough, all demanding premium markups for solving the Big Dig's crisis du jour. We're sure that some $500 hammers and $300 screwdrivers were deemed essential for completing the project. In any case, the politicians were clever enough to ensure that the federal government picked up most of the tab for the difference. And we know this wasn't the first hefty cost overrun in a federal project, nor will it be the last.

As for travel times, there is no doubt that they will improve, at least for the first few months that the underground Artery is open. The Massachusetts Turnpike Authority already says that morning commuting times between Braintree and the Tunnel have dropped from 25 minutes in 1998 to 22 minutes today. (The 3 minutes of savings comes to about $5 billion per minute.) But we don't think that permanent reductions in commuting times are any more likely than Larry Bird putting his Celtic uniform back on. This is because of the law of equal traffic suffering, as first outlined by noted philosopher and one-time Red Sox pitcher Bill "Spaceman"

Lee. The law says that traffic will be attracted to any new increase in roadway capacity, until all routes to all destinations are equally slow. In layman's terms, whatever route you pick will be slow, so don't agonize over it. Use your Boston Driving skills to mitigate the situation.

What about the plans to build a park on the site of the old (elevated) Artery? The designs for the Rose Kennedy Greenway are being debated. Whichever is chosen, there's a real chance here of beautifying the city. Now that's not saying much, because the elevated Artery is about as picturesque as a nineteenth-century steel mill. However, Boston Drivers will never get to see it, because they'll be underground—fighting off each other with deadly maneuvers and breathing too much raw car exhaust to have any chance of having a good day.

So was it worth all the construction hassles and congestion in the 1990s? Of course! A good deal of the project was federally funded, which means it was paid for by North Dakota wheat farmers and

The Rose Kennedy Greenway: not very Rose, not very Green . . . yet

Seattle coffee drinkers, among others. Relatively few American taxpayers outside of New England will ever venture into the Central Artery Tunnel, so it belongs to Boston Drivers to use and abuse. Of course, Boston Drivers have helped fund their share of federal projects of great significance elsewhere in the country, including the world-renowned Paul Bunyan National Historical Park in North Dakota, which is so important to those same wheat farmers. So it all evens out in the end.

So here's a salute to the Big Dig, the lasting legacy of Tip O'Neill, the construction project so ambitious that it makes the digging of the Panama Canal seem like a weekend at the beach!

Dealing with the New Layout Downtown

Three things in life are certain: death, taxes, and backups on the Fitzgerald Expressway. With the construction now winding down, it is important to look at what will happen to the neighborhoods through which the underground Artery will be flowing. While the Big Dig will release a good amount of land for parks, small buildings, and tourist facilities, it's a fair bet that none of it will be used to facilitate traffic flows. Parking spaces and garbage dumps that used to be found next to the elevated Central Artery are long gone. This section will give you an idea of the many problems you are likely to see in traversing the streets surrounding the Artery.

Faneuil Hall Area

We think this will be the toughest part of town to navigate through, a top-notch challenge for the most seasoned of Boston Drivers. To make matters even worse, the continued popularity of Quincy Market and the North End will keep pedestrian traffic at mob levels. The only bright spot is that traffic in the Callahan Tunnel will fall to levels not seen since the 1950s, as many drivers won't be able to find it, and those who know where it is will have difficulty getting to it.

Southbound underground Artery, not quite complete

On-street parking in the Faneuil Hall area will be a big challenge, as the areas underneath and beside the elevated Artery are long gone. To cope with this (without abandoning your car to the indignity of public transportation), we suggest a leisurely tour through the North End to stake out your favorite fire hydrants and no-standing zones. You might, after all, get away with it. In any case, you have little to lose because the fine won't cost much more than a parking garage. Don't bother with the Resident Only parking spaces; they'll be gone before you get there.

South Station

The South Station area took a big hit from construction-related disruption, as bad as or worse than Faneuil Hall. The northbound underground Artery was built about a quarter mile east of the brief underground section of the old Artery, and managed to tear up a lot of the area, in addition to slowing traffic down to miserable levels.

The good news is that South Station is bound to have a major renaissance once the mess is cleaned up. Traffic flow will improve, tourists will come back due to the proximity to the new Boston Convention and Exposition Center, and the southern end of the Rose Kennedy Greenway will add some park space. Experts that we are, we highly recommend pulling the nickels out of your favorite mattress and investing in South Station real estate.

The northbound Artery on-ramp for South Station is near the Moakley Bridge, while the southbound on-ramp is off Kneeland Street. Uncharacteristic of most parts of Boston, these entrances are easy to find and well-marked from all the major nearby streets. The two entrances are spaced about a half mile apart, and nowhere near the corresponding exit ramps off the Artery. Building four separate ramp complexes for this area was one of the many innovative ways in which costs were overrun by $12 billion.

South Boston Piers

The construction of the I-90 extension and the Ted Williams Tunnel carved up this part of town pretty badly in the late 1990s, but that's all over now. Traffic generally flows smoothly in this area, mainly because there are very few reasons why anyone would want to go there. Once the new Convention Center opens, however, there will be merciless gridlock due to the inadequate capacity of the roadways that feed this part of the city. If you plan to attend a convention or trade show at the new facility, you may be there a while, so make sure you bring a sleeping bag and wilderness survival gear.

Logan Airport/Ted Williams Tunnel

While perennial construction projects at Logan Airport always make it look like a war zone, most of the Big Dig construction was on airport property not generally accessible to the public. If you're going to the Harborside Hyatt Hotel or dropping off a few tons of air cargo, then you'll be passing through the new areas; otherwise you might not know they were there.

The entrance to the Ted Williams Tunnel appears as a portal into the underground world, visible from several points on the elevated roadways of Route 1A and the departure side ramp at Logan. The combination of the bronze plaque of Ted Williams at the tunnel threshold plus the lighted yellow glow of the interior will give you the impression that you are entering a shrine.

Once in the tunnel, you'll marvel at how well lit, clean, and empty it is. Apparently old habits die hard, and Boston Drivers are much more comfortable in the grimy, exhaust-laden environment of the Sumner and Callahan Tunnels. We are certain that eventually the word will get out, and Ted Williams's name will be associated with just as much dirt, slime, and congestion as are those of Lt. William F. Callahan, Jr., and William H. Sumner.

Ted Williams's shrine under Boston Harbor

Northbound Leonard P. Zakim Bunker Hill Bridge

Other Words of Wisdom

The new underground Central Artery is not simply a successor to the old elevated structure. One major difference is that the old Artery had twenty-seven exits between Mass. Ave. and the Charles River, while the new Artery will have but three. We imagine that the number of exits was cut so drastically in order to discourage local trips that add to congestion but could be satisfied just as easily on surface streets. However, that makes it more difficult for Boston Drivers. We have already heard reports of unsuspecting drivers who wanted only to go from one downtown location to another and found themselves whisked to Somerville with no opportunity to appeal. In fact, if you don't keep your wits about you, you will end up in Concord, New Hampshire, before you know it.

Finding a suitable on-ramp to get onto the Artery will be an even bigger challenge than finding your exit, because there won't be very many of them. Unlike the hometown highways of yesteryear, there isn't necessarily an entrance that corresponds to each exit ramp, nor will there be the same entrances on the northbound and southbound sides. The bottom line is that you can't simply count on getting back on where you got off. There are a mere three ramps between Interstate 90 and the Charles River that will take you onto the northbound Central Artery/Tunnel. These are located on Congress Street by the new convention center, on Atlantic Avenue by the Moakley (Northern Avenue) Bridge, and on Sudbury Street near Haymarket Square. Boston Drivers who fail to give some forethought to exactly where they want to get on or off the new roadway will get a more complete tour of the downtown area than they bargained for.

4

Basic Maneuvers

In the previous chapters you have seen some of the necessary ingredients for being a motorist in the Boston area today. You now have (or should have) a beat-up car and minimal insurance. The streets are just waiting for you to drive on them. You are mentally prepared to confront the inconveniences of the Big Dig. We are now ready to discuss some of the basic offensive driving techniques you will need to survive as a motorist in this city. This chapter covers some of the most popular and useful maneuvers.

The Cutoff

The cutoff is the most frequently used Boston Driving maneuver. It is used in merge and lane change situations where there is too much congestion to enter the traffic stream easily. When two lanes merge into one, something has to give, and it might as well not be you. In these situations, you must choose a victim, establish a positional advantage, and move far enough into the lane so that the other driver cannot pass you (i.e., the victim is cut off). It is then a simple matter to move fully into the lane, ahead of the opposing driver. This is the essence of a cutoff.

A cutoff may be done from either side. It is somewhat more effective from the right because the other driver is less likely to see

The Cutoff

1. Overtake other car.   2. Edge into other lane.   3. Take over lane.   4. Finish.

a maneuver from the right. Good acceleration and braking capabilities are a definite plus, since some power and precision are required. The cutoff is more difficult with a big car because of its lesser maneuverability, but it is also more effective because of the car's intimidating bulk.

The ultimate in intimidation, we suppose, is your run-of-the-mill MBTA bus. Having no scruples whatsoever, bus drivers will not hesitate to let you know who's boss. Fighting a cutoff from a bus is like trying to find a parking space in Kenmore Square on the night of a baseball game. To add insult to injury, the bus will generally belch a big cloud of black smoke directly at you as it accelerates away.

To execute a cutoff, you must be slightly ahead of the other driver or you will not be able to edge into the other lane. There must be enough clearance between your victim and the car in front of him or her for you to force your front end into the other lane; a car-length is usually sufficient.

The possible defenses against the cutoff follow from the previous points. Ride as close as possible to the car ahead of you. With half a car-length of clearance at moderate speed, it is practically impossible to be cut off. Of course, if the car in front of you decides to brake, you both turn into hamburger, but try not to let that bother you. One way to minimize this risk is to cover the brake with your left foot. That way, you are ready either way. Avoid letting other cars overtake you, for they will then be in a position to cut you off. It might be wise to keep your options open by launching a preemptive cutoff strike against a driver whom you suspect might be thinking about executing a cutoff against you.

The Sidesqueeze

The sidesqueeze is similar to the cutoff, but it is done from the side of your victim rather than by moving in front. To pull off this maneuver, edge slowly closer to the opposing car. The other driver cannot afford to gamble that you really know what you are doing, so sooner or later he or she will have to brake to prevent you from colliding, in case you really have lost your marbles. When this happens, move forward as quickly as possible and take your adversary's lane when you have enough room.

You must be even with or slightly ahead of the other car; otherwise, that driver can counter by accelerating ahead of you when you try to sidesqueeze. You must also be going at about the same speed

The Sidesqueeze

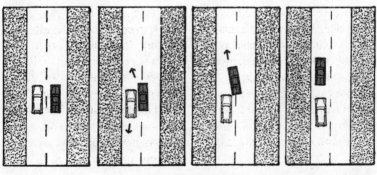

1. Pull even with other car.

2. Squeeze into other lane.

3. Follow through.

4. Finish.

as the other car to produce the proper intimidation effect. It helps to look just a little bit unstable in driving down the road. Don't make eye contact with anyone; if the other driver knows you've seen him or her, you've lost. If you follow this advice, you may be able to convince opposing drivers that you are drunk or incompetent in which case they will almost always get out of your way and let you do anything you want.

Blocking

You will often be confronted with situations in which you're not sure whether you want to be in the left lane or the right lane. This can happen when you are unfamiliar with the road, or searching for an address, or perhaps looking for a parking space on either side of the street. In such situations, blocking becomes a very valuable skill.

Blocking is accomplished by straddling two lanes of traffic. The lane marker, if there is one, should be right under the middle of your car. The advantages of straddling the two lanes should be obvious. No other car can get by you because there is not enough clearance on either side. And you have the flexibility to move left or right once you make up your mind which lane you want to be in. It helps to have a big car for this maneuver, since with a small car, other small cars might still be able to get by. However, you can simply sidesqueeze them if they make any threatening moves.

Blocking

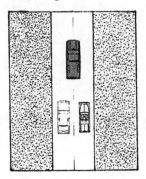

Don't try to extend a block to three lanes: even novice Boston Drivers can easily break up a three-lane block. Just pick a pair of adjacent lanes to block and hope for the best should you eventually need to get into the third lane. Especially if you are looking for parking, you will be going more slowly than the traffic behind you, and you are likely to be on the receiving end of horn blasts, tailgating, high beams, and four-letter words, as these drivers attempt to express some dissatisfaction with your behavior. It is no cause for concern, because you hold all the cards. They cannot pass by you until you let them, and there is no reason to let them intimidate you into doing so.

Intersection Techniques

Where the entire town may be the driver's battlefield, intersections are surely the "front lines." Just as battles are won and lost in the trenches, the nitty-gritty of Boston driving takes place at intersections. About half of all trip time in city driving is spent waiting at or passing through the city's intersections. Cab companies, in particular, are so riddled with intersection accidents that one company automatically assigns fault to a driver involved in one of these. So watch out! All it takes is one little bit of bad timing for a can't-miss introduction to a fellow motorist.

Lights

Many years ago, local authorities decided to regulate traffic flow by placing alternating colored lamps at troublesome corners. Since for every action there is a corresponding reaction, motorists in Boston have nobly responded to the traffic signal with every conceivable ploy, all of which may be summarized by the phrase: "Paint the town green."

If the light is green, obviously you go. And quickly too, before the light changes. But suppose you have been waiting at a red light which suddenly becomes green. Do you gas it forward now? Not in this town you don't, unless you are in a chrome-eating mood. To be sure, your green light means a red light for the cross-traffic, but red lights do not stop most Boston Drivers, at least not right away. We feel that a count of "one one thousand, two one thousand, three one thousand" should be sufficient to allow you to proceed safely.

Alert Boston Drivers will condition themselves to react automatically to the yellow light. The yellow follows the green, lasting

Go, but do not enter.

several seconds before giving way to the red. This signal tells you that your green time is almost up and that you should speed up if possible, or else you will be caught waiting through another light cycle. Missing a light by a second or two may prove more costly than you think, as they are often "synched." Failing to keep in one set of greens could leave you back at Kenmore Square while the more alert motorists cruise halfway to Cleveland Circle. It is worth pointing out that regardless of the circumstances, if the car in front of you foolishly stops on yellow (no doubt an out-of-state driver), it is a good idea for you to stop as well. Similarly, if the car behind you has no intention of stopping, by all means keep right on going.

One of the cardinal rules of driving is surely "Stop on Red." However, if the light is red for more than five seconds, you can assume that it is broken. You may proceed after a quick check for cross-traffic and police cruisers.

If there is no threatening cross traffic, or if you are feeling lucky, it is very helpful to know precisely when your red light will turn green so you can accelerate immediately (assuming, of course, that there are no cars that intend to run the red light in the cross-direction). The best way to do this is to watch for the Yellow Cross Glow. The light from the cross street turns from green to yellow just a few seconds before your light turns green. When you spot the Yellow Cross Glow, get on your mark and get set for your green is only a moment away.

COMMANDMENT 5

Thou shalt look both ways before running a red light.

Bad traffic often makes it difficult to apply many of these tips. One specific case occurs when you have the green with nowhere to go but into the rear bumper of the car in front of you. How frustrating! Traffic is backed up right to the opposite side of the intersection. The only rational relief is to go anyway. Fill any available space in the intersection even if it leaves you sitting in the middle of it. It's either you or the other guys. If you don't move up, everyone else will, leaving you behind to sit through another red light. This maneuver is illegal, but enforcement is nonexistent. If you don't believe that, prove it to yourself some evening rush hour at Berkeley and Newbury Streets.

Massachusetts was one of the last states in the United States to pass legislation permitting right turn on red. As soon as the measure became law, "No Turn on Red" signs began appearing on every street corner. The reason for this was that the traffic planners thought that driving conditions were chaotic enough as they were; adding right turn on red, they felt, would only make things worse. Some of the state legislators from the Boston area were genuinely embarrassed that Massachusetts was so far behind the rest of the nation on this issue, especially in view of the fact that their state had normally taken the lead in traffic law innovations. To make up for this, they are now gathering support for a new law permitting straight ahead on red, and there is a chance that it will pass this year. The Association of Massachusetts Junkyards, currently the most enthusiastic supporter, confidently predicts that straight ahead on red would lead to a 50 percent increase in scrap metal sales in the first year alone.

Arrows

There are times out there when it seems you don't even need to know which way you're going. That's how many traffic arrows are winking at you: left, right, straight. These are devices which thoroughly riddle the newcomer. Arrows, like lights, come in three colors. In theory, arrows only apply to vehicles heading in the direction to which they point. Complicating matters is the fact that green arrows are often used together with ordinary red lights—right on the same traffic control device.

There is an easy way through all this confusion. If any green arrow is on, you may go in any direction you like. That's all there is to it. Any further analysis is a waste of time. Red and yellow arrows, on the other hand, are so rare that they have been labeled an endangered species. Should you come across one, let logic be your guide. Don't proceed in the direction of the red arrow, and you should emerge unscathed. If you are totally confused by rainbow-colored arrows, you always have the option of waiting for them to go away or change to green.

Basic Left Turns

Because of their unique problems, few areas of Boston driving offer more potential for creativity than left turns. Taking a left turn almost always means crossing the oncoming lane of traffic. At intersections cars will occasionally back up in the left lane, as only a few can make their left turn each light cycle. These are just a few examples of the problems you will encounter in the course of making left turns.

If there is no light, both lanes of cross-traffic must be clear before you can take your left turn. A basic solution for this problem is the Boston Left Turn, a technique developed long ago by an

Allston cab driver. You first wait for the left-to-right traffic to clear. Then edge halfway across the road until the other lane clears. If any cars come from your left while you are waiting, that is just too bad for them. Make sure the front of your car is right on the center line so that no cars on your left are tempted to pass in front of you. You won't care if they choose to pass behind you, since they will not be in your way in that case.

The Beat the Green technique is a slightly more elegant maneuver. It is used when you are first in line for a left turn at an intersection with traffic lights. When the light turns green, floor the accelerator to make your left before the oncoming traffic catches up to you. An advanced version of this technique can be observed at the Gilmore Bridge every rush hour. The first few drivers turning left from the O'Brien Highway onto Land Boulevard have the benefit of a left

The Boston Left Turn

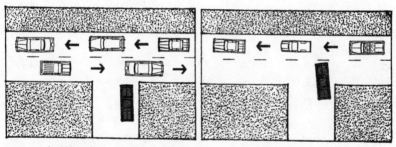

1. Wait for a break.　　　　2. Go halfway.

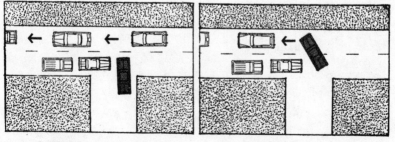

3. Wait for cross traffic.　　　　4. Finish left turn.

Beat the Green

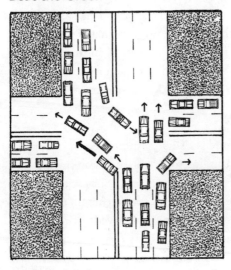

turn signal. But the signal stays on for a woefully brief period of time. Savvy left-turning drivers won't allow a minor detail like the loss of the left turn signal to stop them from making their turn and continuing on their way. Using the preceding car as a screen, they beat the green signal that has now come on for the oncoming cars by cutting to their left. The following car does the same thing, and the process continues until there is no more space to squeeze into. About four cars can usually get through this way without any help from the left turn signal.

Even after all the space is gone, you may still be able to follow the "Green Beater." If the car in front of you Beats the Green, the oncoming traffic must stop. But if you tailgate the Green Beater, they will have to stop for you as well, as long as you can manage to follow so closely that oncoming cars cannot cut you off. Properly done, you will have negotiated a difficult intersection at no greater cost than an earful of horn.

Stop and Yield Signs

Stop signs bring you news that is the opposite of what you want to hear. The eight-sided red banner is an ugly sight to any Boston Driver. But take heart: it is not as bad as it seems. A full stop, though required by law, is seldom necessary. In many cases it is plain that there is no cross-traffic long before the driver reaches the intersection. In others, such as the entrance to Storrow Drive from Beacon Street just before Kenmore Square, the intersection is so blind that there is no point in stopping at all. If you choose to make the turn just as a car comes around the corner in your lane, you will be glad that your car is fully depreciated and your life insurance is paid up. Most intersections lie somewhere in between. In general, slow down only as much as you feel is necessary to stay on top of the situation.

Four-way stop intersections are relatively uncommon in Boston. However, they are a Boston Driver's dream. Since the cross traffic must stop for their stop sign, there is no reason for you to stop also. Just take advantage of your red carpet situation.

By now it should be apparent that the triangular yellow yield signs are a waste of our nation's natural resources. A yield sign theoretically means "stop if necessary." No self-respecting Boston Driver would so much as lift a toe off the gas for a yield sign. This sign, along with its cousin the flashing yellow light, are two traffic control devices that do little to control traffic.

COMMANDMENT 6

Thou shalt not yield.

Rotaries

Most visitors to Boston are surprised to find that a sign marked "Rotary" does not indicate the presence of the local Rotary Club. Rather, it forewarns the seasoned Boston Drivers that they are about to enter a traffic circle. Rotaries are the epitome of anarchy and chaos on the streets of greater Boston. Seen from above, the rotary

looks like a giant centrifuge, spinning cars away from its center at an amazing rate. Those legendary cows who engineered the street layouts back in the seventeenth century are surely rolling over in their graves.

The Massachusetts Motor Vehicle Code says that the cars already in the rotary have the right of way over cars entering the rotary, but don't let that fool you. The code also says that rotaries are intersections, and at an intersection, the car on the right has the right of way. Since the car on the right is always the car entering the rotary, it is far from clear who has the "rightest" way of all. As we have learned, the motor vehicle law has little bearing on what actually goes on anyway. In Boston's rotaries, position is everything: it depends on the configuration of the rotary whether the cars entering the rotary or those already in it have the upper hand.

If the rotary is a large one, there will often be a relatively clear "speed-up" lane to the outside. It is usually easy to enter the rotary, keeping to the right as you accelerate. When up to maneuvering speed, sidesqueeze your way into the main traffic stream.

A very reliable way to enter a rotary in heavy traffic is to use a screen. This can be done if at least two lanes of traffic feed into the rotary. Get into the right feeder lane and concentrate on the car to your left; don't worry about the traffic already in the circle. When your left-hand opponent enters the rotary, follow him or her alongside to the right thereby using the other car as a shield against the traffic already in the rotary. Once you are in, you will be in an excellent position to cut the other driver off, or you can just continue to the right if it suits your purposes.

Once inside the rotary, you will find that the only rule is that there are no rules. There is no protocol for lanes or lane changes because there are no lanes. A good rule of thumb is to keep to the middle, especially if you are unsure where to get off the rotary. If you keep too far left, you will find it difficult to exit; if you keep right you will get murdered by the crossfire of cars entering and exiting the rotary. On the right you are also a sitting duck for being cut off. Keep in mind that since there are no lanes, a fine opportunity exists to practice several of the basic maneuvers described in this chapter. Just remember to look for any daylight between cars.

One word of caution is in order, however. Don't get so wrapped up in your positional struggle that you forget to exit. While it can be quite entertaining to spend an afternoon orbiting around a rotary, life shouldn't be lived that way.

Using a Screen

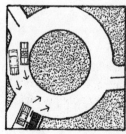

1. Start.

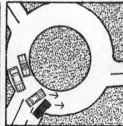

2. Move right when adversary moves.

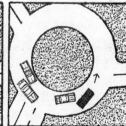

3. Cut adjacent car off if desired.

Weaving

Weaving is the only possible way to move through a heavy traffic stream faster than the flow. While it is most easily done on the highway at high speed, weaving is possible even in stop-and-go traffic, on any road with two or more lanes in each direction. Weaving is an excellent Boston Driving exercise because it requires execution of many of the basic maneuvers described in this chapter.

You must be going at least 10 m.p.h. faster than everybody else to be considered doing good weaving. You execute a series of cutoffs and sidesqueezes. You will have to pass cars on both your left and your right as you move along. As in the case of the rotary, go for the clear lane and take on the passing problem one car at a time.

As traffic becomes heavier, weaving becomes more and more difficult because the required passing space becomes harder and harder to come by. In this situation, cars will often be riding side by side at high speed, and some strategy is necessary to break them apart so you can pass them. The easiest way to solve this problem is simply to wait for a break, since two cars seldom go at the same speed for long. Pull behind the pair and block out other traffic. When one car starts edging ahead of the other, pull behind the faster car and start tailgating: this should speed everyone up. If not apply pressure by turning on your high beams and blowing your horn. When you are even with the slower car, sidesqueeze it and proceed at full speed to pass the faster car. This technique often works even when the two cars are going at the same speed. In general, the larger of the two cars in tandem will be more apt to respond to the type of harassment described above. Cadillacs, in particular, are pushovers.

Beat the Guillotine

Another common maneuver is known as "Beat the Guillotine." In this case, there is a slower car and a faster car ahead of you. The faster car is overtaking the slower, but the faster car isn't going all that fast. Your job is to pass the faster car and cut it off to put you

Beat the Guillotine

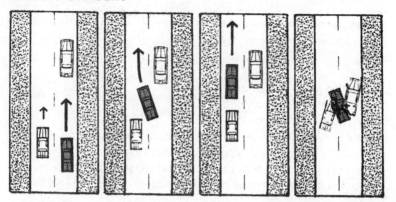

1. Pass faster car. 2. Cut it off. 3. Pass slower car. 4. But don't get
                                                              guillotined!

in position to whiz by the slower car. But if your timing isn't very
good, the faster car can be so close to the slower that you have no
room for a cutoff. In this case your choice is either to give up and
pull back, or proceed with the cutoff and risk being guillotined.

Tailgating

If you can read the newspaper sitting in the back window of the car
in front of you, you are tailgating. The driving school rule of main-
taining one car-length space for each ten miles per hour of speed
does not apply. Boston Drivers routinely maintain a one to three
car-length separation at 60 m.p.h. Besides, safety considerations
have no bearing on the behavior of a skilled Boston Driver.

Although tailgating can be used for harassment, this is not one
of its primary uses. The major advantage of tailgating is that you
cannot be cut off. This is important in heavy traffic or if you are trying to follow someone. Tailgating can be used to communicate to
other drivers that their speed is not up to snuff, and to pressure
them to either accelerate or yield to you. It can also be useful in
jockeying for position during weaving situations.

The disadvantages are numerous, however. Tailgaters can still be sidesqueezed. In addition, once you are tailgating, you are not in a position to pass if such an opportunity should arise. If the car in front of you slows down, you must slow down, and at a slower speed you will have more difficulty changing lanes. All in all, tailgating should be executed only when necessary, for it is a difficult Boston Driving technique of limited usefulness. Blocking is often a much more effective technique for preventing cutoffs.

One-Way Streets

Sooner or later, someone will give you some directions telling you to turn down a one-way street the wrong way. "Don't worry," you are told. "Everyone does it." And everyone *does* do it. Although one-way-the-wrong-way presents certain hazards, it is a valuable tool, because it is often the fastest way to get there, and sometimes the only way.

Occasionally, another car will have the audacity to come down the street the right way, and this might cramp your style, since most one-way streets are only one lane. If you are unable to convince the other driver that the one-way sign has been turned around, you will have to pull over to the side into a parking space or next to a hydrant or driveway and wait for the other car to go by.

It used to be said that unless you were a bona fide daredevil, driving the wrong way on major downtown through streets such as Newbury or Tremont was probably a bit too big a challenge. However, Berkeley Street is enjoying a renaissance of one-way-the-wrong-way driving since Boston Police Headquarters has been relocated from Berkeley Street to Harrison Avenue in the South End. The old Boston Police Department site is being converted to an upscale hotel. Boston Drivers can be expected to show no respect for the preferred traffic direction on the hotel's circular driveway.

One final point: A foolproof way of negotiating a one-way street the wrong way is to go in reverse. That way, you're not heading the wrong way at all.

U-Turns

Because of mistakes in navigating, it is often necessary to make a U-turn. The first thing to remember is that "No U-Turn" signs have all the validity of a three-dollar bill. They were put there to discourage Cadillac owners from tying up traffic for half an hour while they taxi their massive hulks back and forth ten times before finishing. For the seasoned Boston Driver, U-turns anywhere, anytime, present few problems.

On a residential street with little or no traffic, just make the standard three-point turn. Make sure there is not enough clearance between you and the parked cars on the other side that a passing car might try to get by.

On a busy street with lots of traffic, get into the left lane. Signal a left turn; then move a half lane to the right to give yourself a little extra room. This will confuse everybody. It will also discourage anyone from trying to sidesqueeze you at least until they figure out what you are up to. Try to make the turn in one quick swoop. If there is traffic in the other direction, you will be facing across the road when you stop. It helps to have a driveway or an empty side street to help you through the turn. Now all you have to do is cut someone off to get back into the traffic stream.

With less traffic, the U-turn should be done from the right lane. Signal a right turn and pull over to the curb. If necessary, use your flashers. When the traffic clears, make the U-turn. Plenty of room. You can even cross a shallow median this way.

And then, when all else fails, there's always the old reliable gas station U-turn. Take a left into a gas station or parking lot and then pull out of the other entrance to the station back onto the road.

Bad Traffic Situations

Traffic is almost always heavy in Boston, just as it is in most major American cities. For those all-too-common situations where you wish you were walking, make sure you are equipped with an extensive vocabulary of four-letter words, a loud and well-tuned horn,

Busy Street U-turn

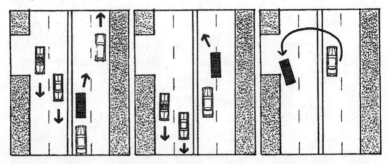

1. Get in left lane and signal left turn.

2. Move half lane to the right to get extra room.

3. Make turn in one motion, without stopping.

and a copy of the *Boston Globe* to pass the time in case the traffic doesn't break.

Merge Techniques

When two lanes of traffic suddenly turn into one, someone (or something) has to give. It is a good Boston Driving technique to make sure neither you nor your car does the giving.

Most merge situations require a straightforward application of a cutoff or sidesqueeze. The problem is that another driver will be trying to do the same thing. As a result, the merge becomes a game of chicken. The loser is the first one to yield. There is bluff and counter-bluff, and the game has many of the characteristics of a military campaign. Looking at some of those battle-scarred bumpers going in and out of the Callahan Tunnel, you'd think there surely had been a war.

There are several things you can do to improve your chances. First, it pays to psych yourself up. Pretend you just got fired from your job. Or the Sox just traded Nomar Garciaparra for two minor leaguers. Now look at the other drivers. It's all their fault. You can see the guilt in their eyes. You'd rather be dead than let any of them merge ahead of you. That's good. You're getting the idea now.

Second, it helps to have a somewhat beat-up car. If you are worried about getting a dent in your shiny new whatever, you'll choke in any merge situation, and probably get the dent as well.

Breakdown lanes aren't just for breakdowns anymore.

Now that you have the right attitude, plunge right into the merge. Sidesqueeze your main adversary as tightly as possible and move forward when the other driver backs down. Simple, wasn't it? All it took was a little bit of properly channeled aggression. Remember to *stand your ground*. If you give an inch, you have lost the battle. The tougher Boston Driver almost always wins in a merge war because there is little opportunity for any finesse.

COMMANDMENT 7

Fear not the merge into heavy traffic, for thine enemies will turn chicken and be vanquished.

On the Highway

Commuter expressways often have special wrong-way lanes at rush hour reserved for carpools. In theory, at least three people must be riding in the car to use this special lane. Since most cars have at most one passenger besides the driver, this lane is usually uncrowded and provides rapid transportation. There is no reason whatsoever why you need to have three people in your car to use this lane. The police could pull you over and give you a ticket but they will never do so because the lane will be blocked if they stop you. Since this would defeat the purpose of the special lane, they have to let you get away with it. If you feel especially paranoid about it, just bring along a couple of well-dressed mannequins.

In bumper-to-bumper situations on major expressways, do not hesitate to use the breakdown lane. We do not understand why this technique is not even more popular than it is. You zoom along unhindered and simply cut off whenever you want to get back into line.

Emergency Vehicles

Lady Luck has certainly smiled on you if a police car, ambulance, or fire truck comes your way while you are stuck in traffic. Most drivers pull over to the right when they see the bubble gum machine and hear the siren, but in bad traffic, there isn't room for everyone to pull over to the right, so the cars in the left lane pull to the left. This looks like the waters of the Red Sea parting. The emergency vehicle goes by, and you just pull in behind it. If you tailgate properly, you can follow it right through the traffic jam. Occasionally as many as ten cars will follow a siren this way. You must act quickly to get on the bandwagon or the Red Sea waters will close, leaving you to drown in traffic along with everybody else. This technique has the added fringe benefit of allowing you to follow the emergency vehicle through red lights, past stop signs, and down one-way streets the wrong way, as long as the location of the actual emergency is not out of your way.

Sure-Fire Bumper-to-Bumper Situations to Avoid

Prevention is surely the best medicine. It is better to avoid a traffic jam entirely than to have to maneuver your way out of one. It pays to be aware of some specific times and places where you should not drive. A few examples:

1. The Fitzgerald Expressway during rush hour on a rainy Friday afternoon—this is where the term "heavy and slow" originated.

2. The Sumner or Callahan Tunnel at rush hour—if you survive the colossal merge, you'll be asphyxiated in the tunnel.

3. Saturday afternoon downtown—the pedestrians will mow you down.

4. Memorial Drive and Harvard Square when Harvard is home for football—it's like a black hole: you get sucked in and never come out.

5. Tobin Bridge on a Monday morning—a terrific way to add to your weekend hangover.

6. Summer Saturday mornings on Route 3 South (to Cape Cod)—don't forget your picnic lunch. Or your picnic dinner either.

7. Kenmore Square when the Red Sox are at home—if the Sox are in the pennant race, you might as well double-park on Brookline Avenue and go to the game.

Ways to Reduce Stress While Waiting in Traffic

1. View the orange plastic construction cones as a chance to practice slalom techniques for the next ski season.

2. Count how many cars are behind you. (Never count the cars ahead of you.)

3. Turn on the radio. If the announcer tells you that there's a big backup on the highway, change stations.

4. Call your favorite radio talk-show host on your car phone. Express your dismay at the deplorable state of the roadways around the city.

5. Look for Boston's infamous sewer rats. If you spot one, follow it; natives know the best shortcuts.

6. Read the local papers. Offer to share them with the drivers around you.

7. Fake a heart attack and sail through the traffic in the comfort of an air-conditioned ambulance.

8. Take up knitting.

9. Take up napping.

10. If you want to exit the highway but there's no exit nearby, make your own.

5

Common Obstacles

Potholes, Pedestrians,
and Other Assorted Hazards

No matter how clever you are in trying to reach your destination in minimum time, you are bound to run up against many obstacles that will work against you. The alert Boston Driver should be aware of the typical road obstructions and what can be done about them.

In general, the best course of action is to avoid the obstacle entirely. Go around it, over it, or through it, if possible. Try to plan ahead so as to avoid having to come to a complete stop or being stuck in the wrong lane. If you are in a difficult position, intimidating other drivers might be a way out of your predicament. They just might let you go by, but even if one of them calls your bluff, at least you haven't lost anything.

Pedestrians

Pedestrians are people who have lost their cars. They can be an awful nuisance, especially in quantity. At a busy intersection they can pile into the street in droves, allowing even an excellent Boston Driver no chance to break through the line. Even in good traffic, a pedestrian can often force a stop by simply barging into the street. The

Downtown Crossing: Pedestrian Heaven

Boston Driver has size and speed advantages, while the pedestrian has more mobility plus the right of way, the latter being not particularly useful on the streets of Boston.

Most pedestrians fall into one of three distinct types of personalities, as described below.

Tenderfeet are afraid of Boston Drivers and will scan for an opening in traffic. When they find one, they will race across the street at top speed. This type of person generally presents no problem. They will be long gone before you can even think about reaching one of them. However, Tenderfeet will occasionally misjudge the situation, giving you life or death responsibility over them. Chances are you will brake and spare their lives, especially if you are in a good mood. However, to ensure that this incident does not recur, seize the opportunity to voice your opinion of their behavior as bluntly as possible. Try jamming on the brakes (squeaky ones are a definite plus), and add a blast of horn if desired. Sometimes this will cause Tenderfoot to freeze; even if it doesn't come as close as you can, open your window, and curse briefly but loudly enough for everyone to hear. Properly done, these procedures should result in your pedestrian victims never again hindering you or any other Boston Driver.

Cool Cats act very nonchalantly when crossing the street. This type walks at a slow pace, is never in a hurry, and will never break stride for you without some show of Boston Driving on your part. They will usually stare you down as they cross the street. For this type, stronger measures are required. Head right toward them at full speed and swerve by them at the last minute. Since they will be looking right at you all the way, it is important to make it close. This technique will often persuade Cool Cat to stop or go back to the curb before getting in your line of fire. This approach works equally well on Tenderfeet, since they will run away as fast as they can, never to return.

The third type, known as *Snakes,* also appears relaxed and unruffled by the prospect of crossing the street. However, they will have the further audacity to look straight ahead, or worse, read a newspaper while ambling across the street. Snakes are very clever because they really know everything that's going on. There are probably mirrors in the newspaper. The intimidation maneuvers used for Cool Cats will still work occasionally on Snakes, but a more effective approach is to fight fire with fire. Approach the intersection with *your* head buried in a newspaper, or try carrying on a conversation with someone in the backseat. Turning your head and appearing to be oblivious to the situation is very important. If pedestrians suspect that you are not aware of their presence, they'll usually get out of your way.

At one time or another, a passenger in your car may have offered you "two points if you hit this one." These "points" are awarded explicitly for striking pedestrians. It is not necessary to injure them to obtain points, but a knockdown is required. Points have no value except as a measure of Boston Driving prowess in dealing with pedestrians. Once earned, points remain in your Boston Driving account for life; they can never be taken away. In recent years, there has been some confusion concerning point values for striking certain categories of pedestrians. We have compiled a list of target values that has been sanctioned by the Boston Association for People-Free Streets, the organization responsible for recording points and arbitrating any disputes concerning their values.

Pedestrian Point Values

Typical Able-Bodied Pedestrian	3
Little Old Lady (with raised cane)	2
Little Old Couple	3
Pregnant Woman	2
Baby Carriage (empty)	1
Baby Carriage (with baby in it)	3
Bicyclists	6
Tourists	1
Dogs	$1/2$
Harvard Jock	10
Absent-Minded M.I.T. Professor	2
Policeman	8
Mayor	10
Governor	15
Anyone carrying three or more packages (for each additional package, add $1/2$)	2
Gas Station Attendant	5
Groups of 3 or more people (for each additional person, add 1)	6

Trolleys and Buses

Trolleys and buses would be no more bothersome than big, slow cars if not for the fact that they stop every other second to pick up or drop off passengers. A fortunate fact of life is that trolleys must stay on the tracks, but your car is free to go anywhere on the road-way. If you are blocking a trolley by straddling the tracks, it has only one option: it must stop. You have two—you can stay in the lane on the tracks or move away. Take advantage of this situation because you are in command. Don't be intimidated by the trolley's lights, the tinkling of its bell, or four-letter words from the driver, because there is nothing the trolley driver can do until you are ready to move.

On parts of Huntington Avenue, you will be competing with the Arborway trolleys for road space. They share the road with you, but they are restricted to the left lane, so you can block them easily. With the trolley behind you, its frequent stops for passengers are of no consequence. On Commonwealth Avenue and Beacon Street you will occasionally need to take a left or U-turn across the tracks. If traffic is heavy enough, and you are crazy enough, just turn onto the tracks and wait. Make sure you are fully blocking the tracks so that the trolley driver has no notions of trying to get by you. If you really want to impress the subway commuters, block both lanes of trolley traffic while you are waiting to turn.

The most common public transportation vehicle is the MBTA bus. As long as you avoid getting stuck behind one, their presence on the streets is tolerable. Let one in front of you, though, and you'll be in for a rough time. The least of your problems will be the stench of unburned diesel fuel straight from the bus's exhaust. Worse, you will have to suffer as it stops repeatedly to pick up or discharge passengers. Your progress is completely at the mercy of the bus driver who blocks enough lanes that you do not have room to pass the bus even when it is stopped. To add insult to injury, discharged passengers will often attempt to walk in front of you as they cross the street.

Dogs

A nice way of characterizing dogs in the Boston area is to say they are a bit short on survival instinct. A more accurate way of characterizing

them is to say they are stupid. Nearly all unleashed dogs look at the streets as their personal playground and are completely oblivious to the hazards of the roads. These are, of course, the essential attributes for a good Boston Driver. If dogs could live to be seventeen years old, they could get their licenses and become first-rate Boston Drivers.

Because the dog usually doesn't know what it's doing, there is no maneuver that is guaranteed to get it off the street. A large dose of horn usually turns the trick; however, in recent years many species have become resistant to this treatment. Slamming on the brakes as you pull up to the dog may intimidate it, but it is just as likely to start sniffing up the bugs caught in your radiator grill. If anyone out there knows a sure-fire secret of dog removal, please let us know. At the moment there is no known cure for the common dog.

Parked and Double-Parked Cars

It is mighty frustrating to find yourself in the right lane behind a double-parked car, with an otherwise clear lane ahead of you and gobs of traffic whizzing by on your left. "Why me?" you ask. "What

The Cutoff on Green Light

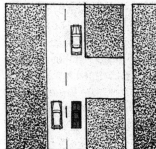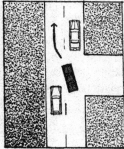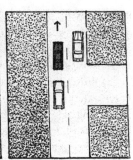

1. Stopped at intersection. 2. Surge forward and execute cutoff. 3. Finish.

did I do to deserve this?" If you are in this situation, you are certainly going nowhere fast. Although you might have to wait for a big enough break in the traffic to switch to the left lane, corrective measures can often be taken.

If you are first in line in the right lane at an intersection with a parked car in your lane on the far side, you might first try the "peace talks" approach. First, take a quick look at the driver to your left and assess his or her Boston driving savvy, taking into consideration the condition of the car, the expression on the driver's face, and the probable state of his or her reflexes. After this, if you feel confident, give some kind of gesture indicating that you would like to proceed through the intersection first. Since you're in a weak position, you'll have to give an Academy Award performance to look like a sympathetic victim.

The blitz approach is usually best. Floor your accelerator as soon as the light turns green and cut off the car in the left lane. This maneuver is very similar to the "Beat the Guillotine" technique described in Chapter IV. It will always work unless the other driver is exceptionally alert; even then, he or she will often let you go anyway, just to be rid of you.

If the left lane traffic has you beaten, pull into the intersection anyway. At worst, you can go when the light turns yellow and the left lane subsequently clears. If someone slows down for a left turn, you've got it made, since the blocking will be done for you. It's one of the few situations where you can shift to the left lane without even bothering to look. This also works if you are caught behind a car waiting to take a left turn.

Similar techniques apply to the problem of pulling out of a parking space into the traffic stream. In this situation don't try any maneuver until you are sure you can clear the parked car ahead of you. It can be very embarrassing to execute a neat cutoff only to find that you have left your front bumper dangling on the rear of the car parked in front of you.

Bicycles

Dealing with pedestrians, trolleys, dogs, and double-parked cars is work enough for the most seasoned of Boston Drivers. But there is yet another obstacle that continues to gnaw away at valuable road space: the bicycle. Bike riders are a strange bunch. They tend to feel very self-righteous about physical fitness, saving energy, and preserving the environment, yet at the same time they fail to realize that they are breathing more exhaust than anybody else. They claim they have a right to be part of the traffic stream, but the truth is they can't cut it in the Big Leagues. Sometimes, they take up enough of the road to slow down traffic significantly, and corrective measures are indicated.

Most bicycle riders, like pedestrians, exhibit one of several distinct personalities, as follows:

Safety Freaks always obey the traffic lights, ride with their hands on the brakes at all times, always keep to the right, and even signal turns. They are religious fanatics, and the Motor Vehicle Code is their bible. Safety Freaks probably own a crackerjack bicycle and the best lock money can buy. At night you can always recognize them by their phosphorescent armbands and enough reflectors to light up

Best place for a bicycle

Copley Square. If one is coming toward you, it will feel like you're staring into a high beam.

In reality, Safety Freaks have a love-hate relationship with the bicycle. Although they derive some enjoyment from the exercise, as all bikers do, they are deathly afraid of cars. They feel inferior because your car is bigger and faster than their bike. The outcome of any showdown between a bike and a car is certain, and they know it. Consequently, they usually suffer from chronic paranoia and expect you to try to swat them like flies.

As a result, this species of bicyclist is beaten before it starts. The slightest sign of aggressiveness on your part will send them scurrying into the shoulder, out of sight and out of mind. Often they will be out of your way long before you reach them. Many Boston drivers have never even been able to take a good close look at this highly elusive creature.

Lefties are a different breed of biker who like to ride on the left side of the road. They usually ride sitting up with one hand on the handlebars. The other hand is unpredictable: it might be doing any-thing on the spectrum of scratching their navels to writing their memoirs. The hand controlling the bicycle is willing to lend itself if necessary to the more executive work being done by the other hand. This leaves nothing steering the bike, but it always seems to keep going straight anyway.

Lefties are intrigued by the thought of watching their own death unfold before their eyes. Riding on the left, they will have full view of the car that makes the hit. If they were to ride on the right, they would likely get hit from behind and would thereby be denied the cosmic experience of watching themselves be killed.

Lefties are more of a hazard to other bikers and pedestrians than they are to cars, but are still a damn nuisance. Lefties think all Boston Drivers are aggressive and malicious toward bicycles (they're right), but they also think they are so much smarter that they can react to any dangerous situation that could develop.

Of course they are wrong, and it is easy to defend your turf as a motorist against any bicycle encroachment. When you see Lefty coming at you, just pull to the right slightly and coax him or her gently off the road. After a few incidents like this, Lefty may be convinced that continuing in this manner could be hazardous to his health. As a general policy, we advocate putting bicyclists in their place: either walking their bikes on the sidewalk or riding them on bike paths, as far as possible from the province of Boston Drivers.

A third type of bicycle rider, known as *Aggressors,* is always racing against the traffic. They usually lose, but that doesn't bother them. As a general rule, they will keep to the far right if they cannot keep up with the cars; at the same speed as the traffic, they will move left to take up a full lane. Given the opportunity, they will pass cars and buses on the left or right, block when it suits them, and weave in and out of traffic. At a light, they will weave to the front of the line, give a quick glance for cross-traffic, and run the light, barely miss-ing a stride. This species of bicyclist pushes their maneuverability advantage to the hilt. Most ride hands on brakes and can stop on a dime. Aggressors are seldom afraid to cut off a car.

If you run into one of these personalities, be aware that you are up against a tough competitor. Aggressors are just about impossible to maneuver into a situation where you can threaten to squeeze them to death between lanes of traffic or between traffic and parked cars. If one blocks your lane, the best thing to do is to try to sidesqueeze him or her to the middle of the traffic stream. This will force the bicyclist to weave and will usually occupy him or her enough to allow you to pass. But beware: a skillful Aggressor will move with you and prevent you from passing.

Potholes

One of the first signs of spring in Boston is the big clank you hear and feel when driving over a pothole. Potholes may be characterized as small pieces of roadway that aren't there. They are consequences of those fine New England winters. The relative warmth of a late winter's day melts the snow and ice on the road, and the water seeps into the pores of the pavement. At night the water freezes and expands, exerting pressure on the road surface and weakening it. The resulting faults in the surface grow bigger and bigger with each passing car until, if nothing is done, a good-sized crater appears on the road surface. There are other sources as well. Many a pothole owes its creation to a hungry snowplow. It is said that Boston has a unique type of plow that scoops up the asphalt while leaving the snow behind.

Most potholes are formed from about mid-February to mid-March. By April Fools' Day the snow has melted, and with it has gone the excess water necessary to form potholes. At this time, the city sends out its maintenance crews to fix some of them. They always run out of money before the job is done, so it's a safe bet that if a particular pothole is still around on Mother's Day it will be there until next spring. Even the chasms that are repaired always have a slight bump where the new asphalt was added. After a few hundred repairs have been made to a stretch of road, it begins to feel like a bed of rocks when you drive on it. Only a complete resurfacing can restore sanity at this point; however, the budget for this type of repair is so small that it takes years before money can be appropriated, and another year or so to do the job.

COMMANDMENT 8

Steer clear of potholes,
for they are the portals of hell.

Where to Find Potholes

Because of the spotty record of the road crews in repairing potholes, it can be quite difficult to predict where you will encounter your next one. Every winter affects each street differently; however, there are a few types of streets that tend to get more than their fair share:

1. *Heavy Traffic Streets.* Potholes can spring up any time on the major streets of Boston and the surrounding suburbs. The constant pounding of bus and truck tires imposes tremendous stress on the road surface, and the slightest little crack in the pavement quickly turns into a voluminous crater. Some potholes are so deep that a car can fall in up to its axle and have to be towed out. It pays to remember where these are located since it can be quite a while before they are repaired.

2. *Industrial Areas.* Again, large trucks take their toll. Since there is little passenger car traffic on these streets, they are allowed to deteriorate to a much worse con-

dition than the more heavily trafficked arteries. While it might seem like a shortcut to sneak by the warehouses of Andrew Square instead of going through typical rush hour traffic, it isn't worth it when you consider that you'll probably need a new set of shock absorbers by the time you finish.

3. *Bridges.* Since their roadways are not supported by Mother Earth, bridges are notoriously vulnerable to pothole formation. As any bicyclist will tell you, it is wise to be aware of these bridge potholes ahead of time, or you run the risk of making a big splash.

4. *Residential Streets.* Although they often don't get too much traffic, residential streets are prime candidates for potholes since they are usually paved with a thinner, lower quality grade of asphalt. Although they don't tend to get very deep, they do tend to stick around for a long time because the lack of heavy traffic gives them a lower priority for resurfacing. Some resourceful folks we know in Belmont are raising a fine crop of tomatoes on what used to be part of their street.

How to Avoid Potholes

1. *Swerve Technique.* If the pothole is seen well in advance, simply change lanes. If someone is already there, do a sidesqueeze. Block if you can, to give yourself the flexibility to swerve to either side.

2. *Straddle Approach.* In this maneuver, the pothole passes harmlessly under the car, between the wheels. This method has the advantage that it is usually not necessary to divide your attention between missing the pothole and cutting someone off. But it requires planning and precise maneuvering to avoid hitting the pothole, especially if it is wider than your front axle.

3. *The "Warp-5" Approach.* If you see the pothole too late and you must go over it, accelerate to the maximum speed possible before hitting the pothole. The theory is that the wheels will "float" over the pothole with minimal damage. The problem with this theory is that unlike the average pothole, it does not hold water. On a bad day, you could lose your front end, transmission, or both. Subscribers to this theory have been seeing too many *Terminator* movies.

4. *The "Easy-does-it" Approach.* In this maneuver, the pothole is once again seen too late to avoid. Slow to the minimum speed possible on the theory that the lower your speed, the less the damage. The problem here is that you can sometimes get stuck if the pothole is big enough and you are going too slowly. Prayer upon crossing the threshold is recommended.

The "Warp-5" Approach

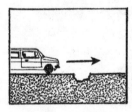  

1. Speed up toward pothole.

2. Remain airborne over pothole.

3. Don't leave anything behind.

Toll Booths

Toll booths are found on only four major arteries in the Boston area: the Tobin Bridge, the Sumner Tunnel, the Ted Williams Tunnel, and the Mass. Pike. A toll booth is the only obstacle that doesn't just slow you down: it detains you until you submit to its blackmail. Unfortunately, the outlook for cash-free alternatives is bleak. The shortest non-toll alternative from the airport to downtown is at least

forty-five minutes longer than the Sumner Tunnel. Similarly, Route 99, with its zillions of traffic lights, is a poor substitute for the Tobin Bridge. And Route 9 is no match for the Mass. Pike.

So face it: you're going to have to pay. Your only choice is whether to pay cash at the designated blackmail point, or become a Fast Lane Tagholder (F.L.T.).

The F.L.T. program allows drivers to establish accounts with the Mass. Turnpike Authority. When you drive through a tollbooth, the account is automatically debited the amount of the toll by means of a Fast Lane Tag affixed to your car. Being able to keep moving through tollbooths is the major advantage enjoyed by F.L.T.s. Of course, if traffic is backed up to any degree, both the F.L.T.s and the cash customers will receive equal shares of frustration.

The F.L.T. program has other downsides as well. While Boston's F.L.T.s are moving through tollbooths with panache and aplomb, few of them are aware of the tab they are running up, as there's no music played or electric shock given every time the cash register goes ka-ching. So if someday your car is repossessed out from under you as you emerge from the Sumner Tunnel, you'll learn (belatedly) that you weren't paying attention to your F.L.T. account.

Those who drive through the Fast Lane without a tag are automatically photographed and hunted down. So if you don't have a Fast

Payment required for admittance to Boston

Lane Tag, don't ever make the mistake of missing the cash payer lane. If you slow down, try to sidesqueeze into the cash lane, or otherwise call attention to yourself to the detriment of traffic flow, you will be subject to severe consequences from bona fide F.L.T.s. Courts have even ruled that homicide can be justifiable under these circumstances. Instead, play it cool, pretend you have a tag, and phone the Mass. Pike Authority as soon as you can to beg for forgiveness. You may not escape the fine, but at least you'll live to drive again.

Trucks

Doing battle with a truck is like taking on the front four of the New England Patriots: if you're lucky, you'll bounce off. On a bad day, they can turn you into a pancake. In spite of bumper stickers that say, "Drive safely," trucks are the only vehicles that will never yield. Why should they? Their survival is never in doubt.

You don't need to see a truck to know that it is coming. Ill-mannered, loud, and foul-smelling, trucks always give ample warning of their presence. However, there is no need to panic at the first sound of the diesel monster. The Boston Driver has two key assets at hand: speed and maneuverability. Like the English Navy that out-foxed the Spanish Armada, the good Boston Driver will easily be able to reduce any truck to a minor nuisance.

Trucks would present little obstacle if not for the truck drivers. Truck drivers are usually men with above average height and weight who look like they haven't seen a shower in a week. Many carry a sticker on the back of their trucks proclaiming: "This vehicle paid $662,523,987.50 [or some other equally ridiculous amount] in road use taxes last year." That, they believe, entitles them to behave as if they own the road. Also, since their vehicles are bigger than anyone else's, they will often drive as if no one else is around. One sticker you probably won't see is one announcing that the truck's driver has paid a like amount in fines for exceeding load limits and other violations of federal and state law. Call that 800-number on the back of the truck to ask just how large this amount is.

Because of their size, trucks should never be taken lightly, and there are a number of pitfalls to beware. If you are tailgating a truck in wet weather, be sure to keep your windshield wipers on, or else be prepared to be blinded and buried under an avalanche of water and mud. If the truck is carrying open cargo, be prepared for an unscheduled delivery directly in front of your car at any moment. Depending on what kind of cargo is being carried, you will have to be prepared to react.

Another especially bad time to be in back of a truck is at a toll booth. Despite the $662,523,987.50 paid in road use taxes, it never fails to take forever for the truck driver and the toll attendant to set-tle up. When it finally does leave the booth, be wary of falling asleep waiting for the truck to accelerate up to speed.

Finally, don't ever let yourself get caught between a truck and the guard rail, for you might end up instantly transformed into a sausage pizza.

6

Parking

Whatever your destination, you will eventually have to park your car. It would be so nice to be able to step out of the car, push a button, and watch the car collapse to the size of a pack of cigarettes. Unfortunately, life is not so easy, and if you're trying to park in front of the Fleet Center on the night of a Stanley Cup playoff game, life can be downright difficult. Even though you cannot fold up your car in George Jetson style, do not despair. Parking in Boston is a challenge that nourishes the creative mind like no other. There are lots of opportunities for the skilled Boston Driver to demonstrate prowess in the quest for a parking space. Although parking is often an annoying hassle, we believe that no one should ever have to avoid driving for fear of not being able to find a free parking space.

Tickets, Tows, and Denver Boots

Every driver is happy to find a legal parking space in a congested area. But many Boston Drivers are unaware of the extra opportunities that illegal parking offers. You can count on lots of spaces to choose from, and you can usually get close to your destination. However, there are certain pitfalls to beware. Although none of these are likely, you can get a ticket. Or towed. Or the worst of all possible fates: the Denver Boot, alias "The Immobilizer."

Tickets range in severity from ten dollars for overnight parking in the suburbs to fifty dollars for rush hour parking on a busy downtown street. Until the mid-'80s, Boston Drivers could throw away parking tickets with impunity. Some drivers even proudly displayed their ticket collections, neatly stacking them in the glove compartment and producing them on request. Others let them dangle from the rear-view mirror, shuffling in the vent exhaust.

Alas, the game is much tougher now. Needing a legitimate source of revenue, in 1981 the city of Boston hired John Brophy to clean up the parking enforcement machinery. Well-credentialed with a Ph.D. in Extortion, Brophy and his lieutenants built a ruthless collection steamroller for the city. Boston now boasts an 83% collection rate on tickets, the highest in the nation. You can still use your ticket for a bookmark, but Brophy's bullies will keep you from renewing your registration and driver's license, and might even boot you in the dead of night.

Which is to say that once you've been ticketed, you've probably lost the battle. But it isn't nearly as bad as getting towed. Sometimes the police will tow if a car is parked illegally on a public street. Most towing, however, is done by private companies whose "clients" are businesses with parking lots. The business makes a deal with the towing company to tow everybody parking in the lot at certain hours (usually overnight). The tow costs you, the vehicle owner, an arm and a leg, a rate regulated by the city and far exceeding the towing company's cost of kidnapping your car. The fee must be paid in cash. No checks please, for you might stop payment. And the companies are not yet progressive enough to take MasterCard. Let's face it: your car is being held for ransom. The excess profits are spent on such things as attack dogs, barbed wire fences, and other security measures designed to prevent you from stealing back your own car.

But even a tow pales in comparison to the humiliation of the ultimate Boston Driving fate—the infamous Denver Boot. Painted a bright yellow color that cannot be viewed without sunglasses, the

Booted in Back Bay

Boot is the modern equivalent to the Scarlet Letter. Like its puritanical predecessor, it's designed to induce a feeling of total humiliation in its victims. But as any Bootee will tell you, the embarrassment comes not so much from being publicly branded as a petty criminal but from the realization that you've been too dumb to avoid getting caught.

The advent of the Boot inspired at least one entrepreneur who monitored the radio frequencies used by the boot squads and identified freshly booted cars. Having zeroed in on his market, he then attached to the car a leaflet promoting his services. For a fee of $25 plus 8 percent of the total outstanding tickets and ransom fees, he would call the police, stand in line to pay the fines, and have the victim's car set free. It's a uniquely lucrative Boston Driving service designed to put cars back in circulation quickly and conveniently so they can resume racking up parking tickets.

The Boot has been successful enough as an intimidation device that it is harder to find on Boston Streets today than five or ten years ago. We can only assume that booted cars in public view have had a deterrence effect similar to the town square hangings of the 1880s.

Resident Stickers

A recent change to the rules of the parking game can be found in several of the residential neighborhoods of Boston and Cambridge, where stickers are required for on-street parking. No longer is it sufficient simply to find a parking space, you also need a *neighborhood identification card* for your car. If you don't have one, you're just as exposed to a ticket as you would be parked next to a fire hydrant.

Resident stickers are not very hard to get. Almost any document with a neighborhood address will suffice as proof of residence, including a driver's license, utility bill, or piece of junk mail addressed to "Occupant." We should point out, however, that if you

choose to pretend to be from the neighborhood, it will help your case immensely to have Massachusetts plates on your car.

Notwithstanding the ease of obtaining a sticker, there is little need to do so because there are no legal parking places anyway. The number of issued stickers is as much as four times the number of parking spaces in some neighborhoods. No one really knows where the other 75 percent of the cars go, particularly overnight. There can't possibly be enough private lots and illegal spaces to absorb them. Maybe there's a storage facility out in the Arizona desert somewhere. Or maybe these autos become part of Boston's extensive car recycling program (see Chapter I, "Insurance").

Resident stickers are a 24-hours-per-day, 7-days-per-week operation. This means no break for Christmas, sales at Filene's, or Larry Bird's birthday. Even the passage of an on-time budget by the state legislature doesn't relax the rules. The inflexibility of all this is a bit tough, particularly for people who regularly entertain visiting heads of state and suburban transients, neither of whom are likely to have stickers. Most neighborhoods have therefore designated about half a block where permits are not required. Assuming you can even find this street, your chances of getting a space are just slightly better than moving Fenway Park to Rhode Island. You'll have better luck looking for a lonely fire hydrant and a trash can with which to cover it.

Is an Illegal Space Right for You?

The alert Boston Driver should bear in mind that there is always a chance of being "caught" when parking illegally. The chances of being caught and the likely consequences should always be taken into consideration. Here are some important questions to ask yourself:

1. *Is it a tow zone?* The likelihood of being towed is an important factor. You should favor spaces that do not impede traffic flow. Some places to avoid are the entrance to the Mass. General Hospital Emergency Room, the center lane of the

Parking "by ear"

Central Artery, and the Governor's space in the State House parking lot.

2. *Are other cars parked nearby?* Parking in a tow zone is a much better risk if there are lots of other cars parked there as well. Being towed is unlikely because the police would have to do the same to everyone else parked in the tow zone. Furthermore, many of the other cars are probably owned by neighborhood residents who know that the area is safe. At worst you will get a ticket, but it is usually worth the risk. On the other hand, if you would be the only car in the no parking zone, beware, for you are begging for the jaws of the tow truck.

3. *How long will you be parked?* For a minute, almost anything goes; for a week, better keep your nose clean. We know of one friend who claims to have double-parked in front of Filene's all day one Saturday (before Washington Street was closed to traffic), but even we find this hard to believe.

4. *How much of a hassle is walking?* If it is pouring rain, or ten below zero, or you are carrying some packages, you will want to get as close as you can. In this case, you would want to pass up a legal space far away from your destination if you can find an illegal one closer in that better meets your needs.

Cruise Techniques

Let's say you are riding down the street looking for a parking space. This is known as cruising. The first rule to remember is to cruise as close as possible to the middle of the street, blocking if necessary, in order to give yourself the flexibility to grab a space on either side. When you see a space on the right, proper procedure is to put on your right blinker, pull over just past the space, and go into reverse. This claims the space for you. If anyone has the audacity to front into the space while you are getting ready to back into it, you should calmly get out of your car and ask the other driver to leave, for he or she has committed a serious breach of parking space ethics. If the other driver refuses, you are then justified in coming back in fifteen minutes and letting the air out of his or her tires, or worse. Fortunately, this type of impropriety is fairly infrequent.

The real challenge in a cruise situation is to grab a space on the left side of a two-way street. The best approach is to have someone in your car stand in the space until you get there. U-turns into a parking space are very hard to execute properly. If you go around the block in order to face the proper direction, the space will usually be gone.

COMMANDMENT 9

Thou shalt grab the first parking place
thou seest, for a second chance will
never come to thee.

Proper fire hydrant parking technique

Do not overlook the possibilities of "quasi-legal" spaces while cruising. Street corners, taxi stands, and crosswalks are technically illegal, but one rarely gets a ticket, much less towed, so these spaces are as good as legal ones. Fire hydrants present another good source of parking spaces. Legally, there must be at least ten feet of clearance on either side of a fire hydrant; in practice, one firehose-width is sufficient. Actually, the best way to handle hydrants is to bring along an empty garbage can, place it upside down over the hydrant and put the cover on top. Nobody, especially the police, will be the wiser. In residential areas, you may be able to "borrow" a garbage can if you don't already have one along. What to do with the trash that may already be in it is a vexing problem. Some have suggested keeping an empty gift-wrapped box in your car for this purpose. Stow the trash in it and leave it on the sidewalk. With any luck, it will be stolen in no time.

Street Cleaning

Parking is banned on some streets for two to four hours each week, allegedly for street cleaning. Most of the time, the street cleaning is not done and no cars are towed. No doubt this does little to improve Boston's reputation that it is not the cleanest city around. Sometimes the street cleaning is done around the parked cars. Once in a *great* while, *everybody* parked in the street cleaning zone will be towed. By the time the street is clear of cars, the two hours are up, parking is legal again, and the street cannot be cleaned. This is the ultimate joke of Boston street cleaning: they can tow you and they don't even have to disturb the slime on the street. Evidently, it is easier to remove thousands of pounds of automobiles than a few measly pounds of dirt.

If you do park in a street cleaning zone, however, you will get away with it almost every time. If possible, park in the middle of the zone; then glance over about ten minutes after the ban goes into effect. If you see tow trucks, you will probably have time to rescue your car before it is kidnapped. If not, congratulations; you are safe for the entire duration of the street cleaning period.

Where to Park

Downtown Shopping Area

Take the subway. During shopping hours there is absolutely no hope, and you may be stuck in traffic. If you are willing to walk across the Common, you can almost always find a space in nearby Beacon Hill, and sometimes it will even be legal.

South Station Area

During business hours, it is very tough. Try finding a metered space on Summer Street just on the other side of the Fort Point Channel. Technically, you will have left the city of Boston in favor of South Boston, but cheap on-street parking is hard to find. Nights and weekends are another story as parking meters are not in effect after hours. So if you can grab a space in Chinatown, for example, you're set for the evening. When picking someone up at the railroad station, just park in front, throw your flashers on, and go inside.

Flashers are always good for fifteen-minute parking—anywhere, anytime.

Government Center/Haymarket/North Station

Ever since the Faneuil Hall redevelopment, finding prime parking spots in this part of town has become a big challenge, and the loss of space under the elevated Central Artery makes the problem worse. If you are fortunate enough to nab one of the few metered spaces, don't fret if you don't have the right change. Considering all the out-of-state cars that converge on this part of town, the police have pretty much given up on parking enforcement in the area. Here, too, once 6 P.M. rolls around, you can breathe easier as the meters are no longer in effect. The limited street parking that once characterized the streets between North Station and Haymarket is all but gone. In its place is an enormous parking structure where spaces abound at 1 Congress Street between New Chardon and

The challenge of parking in the North End turns many drivers upside down.

New Sudbury Streets. Fleet Center event parking is only $17. What a bargain!

For North Station, we can no longer recommend the few illegal spaces that were frequently available on Nashua Street off Leverett Circle, where enforcement was somewhere between lax and nonexistent. Alas, the Suffolk County Sheriff's Department has chosen Nashua Street for its new headquarters building.

Back Bay

Primarily a residential area, much of Back Bay parking is reserved for cars with resident stickers, with a smattering of metered spaces interspersed throughout. Boylston and Newbury, the main commercial streets, feature metered parking. During peak shopping hours, though, divine intervention will be necessary to find any of these spaces unoccupied. Don't worry about overstaying the time limit, because the risk of a ticket ($30) is comparable to the certainty of the cost of a parking garage ($25–$29).

If you value neither your car nor your life, you can slipslide through the rows of stripped cars and mugging victims and park on Back Street. Should your car survive the thieves who hang out there, it will probably be towed. All parking on Back Street is private, and the residents guard their spaces much more zealously than the Boston police ever could.

Theater District

A space can always be found in Bay Village, a small residential area bounded by Stuart, Arlington, and Tremont Streets. The houses look very similar to those of Beacon Hill, and the area seems seedy at first glance. However, rumor has it that the area is, in fact, quite safe, and we are unaware of any pattern of North End–style vandalism in this part of town.

While most of the parking is reserved for cars with resident stickers, a number of spaces are given over to visitor parking. These

Whatever the reason, park elsewhere.

spaces are metered and can typically be found at the ends of blocks. As these meters are only in effect Monday through Friday from 8:00 A.M. to 6:00 P.M., the visitor spaces are ideal for Saturday matinees. The commercial streets in this area (e.g., Columbus Ave.) abound with metered spaces. These meters are in effect from 8:00 A.M. to 8:00 P.M., Monday through Saturday. All these meters will consume your quarters at the rate of $1.00 per hour, with a 2-hour limit.

Kenmore Square

The discussion of Back Bay parking on page 97 also applies to the residential streets around Kenmore. There are meters on the com-

Perpendicular parking

mercial stretches, but such spaces are hard to find except at those odd times when no one is likely to be looking.

If it's the night of a baseball game, you can get away with almost anything. People have been known to double-park on Brookline Avenue. We don't recommend this because even if you don't get towed, you will have a terrible time getting through the hordes of pedestrians that pour into the streets after the game. You might try parking on the Brookline side of Park Circle; it's a fifteen minute walk, but on a nice summer evening, who cares? After the game is over, you must head away from Kenmore Square, even if it means going out of your way. If you don't, you run the risk of sitting in the black hole of post-game cars and pedestrians for quite a while longer than you bargained for.

Brookline Avenue/Hospitals

First try should be the streets between Brookline Avenue and the Riverway. If these don't work you can always cross the Riverside

Brookline's best bargain

Line subway tracks and park on Chapel Street. At fifty minutes for a quarter with a ten-hour limit Monday through Saturday from 8:00 A.M. to 6:00 P.M., Brookline is a breath of fresh air for frustrated Boston parkers. And it's only a five-minute walk from there to the hospitals. But remember, no overnight parking in Brookline.

Harvard Square

Most people think this is toughest park of all. For short-term weekday parking, there are metered spaces on several of the streets leading into the square such as Brattle. These close-in meters are good for one hour. If you're willing to walk a bit farther, you can leave your car for two hours. Enforcement is tough, and at the cost of 25 cents per half-hour, it hardly seems worth it to be a lawbreaker.

A number of office buildings and hotels in the Harvard Square area have private parking garages. People who live or work in these buildings have magnetized cards that get them through the gate. So try telling the attendant you lost you card. Pull into the lot as if you own it. If you have to, you can make up a name for your firm: "Jenkins & Martinez, 6th floor." It helps to be well-dressed and look official. It's a lot easier to convince an attendant than to convince a computerized gate.

Then try Winthrop Street, west of J.F.K. The street is extremely narrow, but if you can get your car onto the sidewalk, nobody will bother you.

Residential streets near the Square are an unreliable last resort. Between Brattle and Mt. Auburn Streets are several cross streets with potential parking, but you are likely to walk a long way even if you find a space. The same problem applies to all streets east of the Mass. Ave./Mt. Auburn Street intersection.

Allston/Brighton

Stop anywhere. Shut off the motor. Lock up. Voila: a safe parking space.

Convenient sidewalk parking

7

Winter Driving

New England winters do not have the greatest of reputations; in fact, they are downright depressing. Proper Bostonians complain almost as much about the wind, cold, snow, and ice as they do about the Tobin Bridge on Monday morning. Winter driving applies to only a few months each year, but it is worth being prepared for the additional hazards and opportunities.

Snow Emergencies

Let's say it is January, and we have just been hit by a nice fourteen-inch nor'easter (pronounced "nawtheastuh"). Now what happens? Well, that depends. If conditions are rotten enough, the mayor will declare a snow emergency. This means that parking is prohibited on certain designated streets in the metropolitan area. At all other times, parking on these streets is perfectly legitimate. Generally, the beginning and end of a snow emergency are announced on all the radio stations. It remains in effect until the city has had a chance to do as much plowing as it feels like doing and then calls it off.

"Snow emergency" is a form of martial law. Boston Drivers have no rights and may be treated very arbitrarily and without appeal. The behavior of the authorities is erratic in snow emergency situations. Most of the time, they will plow around you if you leave your car parked on a snow emergency street, leaving you with a big shoveling job to get your car but not any other inconvenience. Occasionally the plows will deliberately bury your car with all the excess snow on the street You will have to shovel the equivalent of a driveway full of snow to free your car. In this case you will have so much to shovel that you might as well wait for spring.

Because so many people park illegally on snow emergency streets, your chances of a tow are minimal during the day. There is more concern about keeping the streets as clear as possible for business and commuter traffic. The available tow trucks are busy with plowing and freeing stuck motorists and don't have time to deal with scofflaws like you. During the evening and night, however, there is less necessity to keep the streets clear, since there is less traffic, and towing begins en masse. In some of the wealthier suburbs that ban overnight parking to begin with, being towed is just about guaranteed. Make sure your car is off the street before settling down for the evening in front of the boob tube. With the streets clear of parked cars by about 4:00 A.M., the plows need to go over the streets just one more time to have them ready for morning rush hour.

General Street Conditions

Like most things in life, the matter of plowing is mostly a matter of money. In the wealthy northern and western suburbs, equipment is ample, budgets adequate, parking bans enforced, and plowing finished just a few hours after the snow stops. Everywhere else in the metropolitan area, snow budgets would be adequate only if Boston were a tropical paradise. By mid-January (if not earlier), most communities are already dipping into next year's snow budget.

Plowing is fair to good on major streets of downtown Boston, Government Center, Kenmore Square, and most arteries going out to Allston, Brookline, Cambridge, and the major expressways. Parking bans are generally not enforced because of a shortage of tow trucks (see the discussion on snow emergencies above). The plowing job is often sloppy as a result, but the constant crunching of tires on the snow that remains eventually makes up for it.

On the residential streets of Boston and some surrounding communities the streets may not be plowed for two or three days, if at all. These streets are low priority, and there aren't enough plows to do the job any sooner. As for parking bans, forget about them. Nobody is going to wade through fourteen inches of snow to give you a ticket, and the tow trucks will get stuck long before any of them can get their chains on your car.

By no means does the story end when the last plow has cleared the last street. In the suburbs, where an excellent plowing job is usually done, the streets are wide and parking is plentiful. A thin layer of packed snow generally persists, but the crews come back the first warm day with special machines to scrape it off. Such is life in suburbia.

In the major city streets, snow piles up around the parked cars that escaped towing during the snow emergency. This slows up traffic, but not too badly. The snow left by the plows is quickly chewed up by the constant roll of tires on it. The bright sunshine that usually follows a storm contributes as well, no matter how cold the temperature is.

In the case of the lonely residential streets, the storm continues to battle you long after it is over. Snow piles up on all sides of parked cars. If the street was never plowed, a thick "median" will develop on the street. You must drive your car in the snow tracks left by the other cars. If the street was plowed, the packed snow that remains has a habit of turning into ice. Traffic is usually reduced to one lane, and it is slow, slow, slow. If the street is two-way, it may be difficult to get by, as one car may have to pull into a driveway to give passage to an oncoming car. These streets get little traffic or sunlight, so the snow remains around much longer.

Parking Space Entry and Exit Techniques

In Chapter VI we discussed techniques for finding parking. In the winter, there is the additional problem of squeezing your car into the space. This may sound trivial if you have never spent a winter in Boston, but rest assured it can be just as difficult to maneuver your car into two- or three-foot snowdrifts as it is to maneuver out of them.

Certain points of etiquette should be pointed out. The owner of a space during the storm retains "rights" to it for several days afterward because he or she was the one who had to shovel out the space originally. The convention is that a garbage can claims a parking space during the winter. If you are foolish enough to remove someone's garbage can and take the space, you will be a sitting duck for slashed tires, stripping, or any of a thousand other fates you so richly deserve. Without this standard, the parking space could not be protected.

Parking is tight in winter, because so many spaces are lost to the snow. It is considered permissible to box in another car if you have to. If the car you box in cannot get out, that's someone else's problem. If you are the one who's boxed in, however, it is perfectly OK to wipe out a good chunk of the bumper of the car that boxed you in. In the wintertime, all's fair in love and parking.

If the snow is deep, you may not be able to park parallel to the curb. This is no sweat unless you are blocking traffic. Remember

Proper parking space construction

that the traffic lane is much smaller, so you could have one end of your car four feet off the curb and still be OK. Don't block a driveway, though, unless it's only for a minute. If you do, the car is likely to end up on the dinner table of the local neighborhood towing company.

Track-in Approach

The easiest way to get into a parking space is to use the tracks made by the last car to leave. This usually means backing in. Ideally, your car will be about the same width as the tracks. If you're crazy and you have time, energy, and a shovel, you might want to dig out the space, but this is seldom necessary unless the snow is at least a foot deep.

Blitz Approach

A deliberate and accurate approach to winter parking will get you nowhere. If the snow is more than three or four inches deep, you must floor the accelerator in order to build up some speed before crossing into the snow. Once you cross, you're almost sure to lose some control, skid, and probably get stuck. You must park in one move: if you stop, you will get stuck there. Don't touch the brake until you have either safely arrived in the parking space or wiped out the radiator of the car behind you. Don't worry about getting out of the space; save that for when you come back.

Getting Out

The most frustrating feeling that can be experienced by a Boston Driver is to have your car stuck in snow only inches away from the bare pavement on the main part of the road. Until you go those few inches, you don't go anywhere. Escaping is mostly a matter of gravity, friction, shoveling, and praying. But there are a few techniques that can help matters along.

The most reliable method of escaping from snow is to be pushed out. This is one time when there is no shame in getting by with a little help from your friends. Passing pedestrians will almost

Burial victim

The Rock-a-Bye-Baby Approach

1. Accelerate.   2. Rock back.   3. Drive forward and out.

always give you a hand without even being asked. Never refuse anyone's offer: the more hands pushing the car, the merrier.

If there are no other people around, you might try putting some rough material under the wheels to increase traction. Some things to try are sand, an old towel, floor mats, the back seat upholstery, or a Dukakis-for-President T-shirt.

An easy escape from the magnetic snowdrifts is to park facing downhill. Gravity will do most of the work, with a gentle assist from the accelerator. The trouble with facing downhill is that if you get boxed in, you have almost no hope of getting out. If this happens, you should somehow push the other car far enough down the hill to give you the room you need. If all else fails, a series of love taps from your car to the other may persuade it to get out of the way.

If your rear tires are in a rut of packed snow, you may have to use the rock-a-bye-baby approach. Put the car in gear and accelerate until the wheels spin. Now let up on the accelerator, and the car most likely will roll back into the rut. Repeat these two steps, going a little farther each time, until you are out. Having someone to push your car greatly helps. You should be able to time perfectly the movement of the car and the accelerator pressure. Some clever drivers with automatic transmissions can keep shifting in synch from forward to reverse and back again, but this is usually just for show.

If you are stuck and can't free yourself, at least try to maneuver your car far enough into the street to block traffic. You will then find plenty of other drivers eager to help you. Don't worry: they're not motivated by any sort of good intentions; rather, they want to get you on the move so they can proceed themselves.

By far the most common and counterproductive method for extricating oneself is the "dentist's drill" approach. In this method frustrated motorists floor the accelerator so hard that their wheels spin. The more the wheels spin, the harder they gun the accelerator. The harder they gun the accelerator, the more the wheels spin. The dentist's drill can be heard on almost every street in Boston nearly every winter morning.

Don't you make the same mistake. Carried to extremes, the dentist's drill approach creates ice ruts so deep that you might just as well wait for baseball season to get your car out. If the dentist's drill doesn't get you out right away, you will have to stop, shovel some more around the wheels, and accelerate as slowly as possible out of the mess so as to create maximum traction. Just keep your cool, and save the dentist's drill for the dentist.

Winter Maneuvers

Since speed and maneuverability are considerably reduced during winter conditions, there are fewer opportunities to keep Boston Driving techniques sharp. But there are a few maneuvers that apply only to snow and ice that are worth discussing.

Turns

On an icy road surface, it is easy to go into a skid while making a turn. Since the road is so slippery, the steering wheel turns easily whether the car has power steering or not. The front wheels turn, but nobody tells the rear wheels to turn, so they keep going straight and a skid results.

Turns on Ice

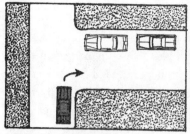
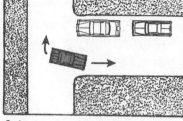

1. Accelerate into turn. 2. Lose control; rear wheels skid.

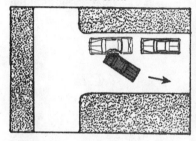
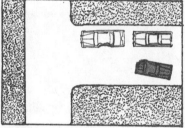

3. Bounce quietly off parked car; 4. Finish.
   regain traction.

The standard driving school technique of turning into the direction of the skid might get you back in control of your car, but this method is clumsy and inelegant because it often leaves you off to the side of the road out of the traffic stream. We favor a blitz approach: when your car begins to skid, hit the accelerator in an attempt to build up enough speed to drag the rear wheels through the turn. Usually the wheels will hit a patch of sand or bare pavement and propel the car forward. Under ideal conditions, you might even burn some rubber. The worst thing that could possibly happen is that you might ram a parked car in a spot where it was already dented.

"Skitchers"

After a snow or ice storm, kids sometimes like to grab the rear bumper of a car when it stops at a light and be towed with their feet sliding along the ice. This is called skitching and is very dangerous for the kids. It is, however, no problem for you. Skitchers are simply aggressive pedestrians and should be treated as such. One thing you might try is coming to a slow stop, then getting out of your car and chasing them away. This is unlikely to convince them who's boss, so more drastic measures are generally called for. We favor a sudden acceleration while pretending not to notice that they're there. This is fighting fire with fire and will usually persuade the skitcher to let go. If all else fails, you can go into reverse to get rid of a skitcher of two, but make sure your license plates are obscured by snow, just in case someone is watching.

One-Way Streets

If you are thinking about going the wrong way on a one-way street during a big blizzard, by all means go right ahead. Since you will be the only one foolish enough to be out on the street in such bad weather, you should have no problems.

Stop Signs and Intersections

On an icy road forget about stop signs, since you can't stop anyway. If the road is covered with thick snow, it is a mistake to stop just because you see a stop sign. If you do so, you may find yourself stuck, or at best it might take a while to accelerate back up to speed. This also applies to red lights, especially at night when all sane persons are already home.

8

Advanced Maneuvers and Harassment Techniques

Having read the first seven chapters of this book, you have acquired all the basic skills necessary to become a first-rate Boston Driver. You could stop right here and drive happily ever after, but you would miss out on some of the fine points that separate the mere expert drivers from the superstars. This chapter describes some advanced maneuvers and harassment techniques that you can use as desired to obtain an edge over your fellow Boston Drivers. Most of the maneuvers described in this chapter are expansions on the basic maneuvers covered in Chapter IV, which should now be a routine part of your Boston Driving repertoire.

Why?

You might wonder why you need to learn to harass your fellow Boston Drivers. "After all," you might say, "they don't harass me." Unfortunately, this simply is not true. Every time you are the victim of a commonplace cutoff, sidesqueeze, or block, you have been harassed. Whenever someone beats you to a lonely parking space or double-parks in your lane of traffic, you have likewise become the object of harassment, intentional or not. There is often very little you can do about this type of treatment. However, the best defense is a good offense: do unto others before they do unto you. Remember, it's nothing personal. You're just playing the Boston Driving game the way it is meant to be played.

Many of the maneuvers described in this chapter are not widely known at present; therefore, we suggest that you use a certain amount of discretion when executing them. Overuse of these techniques could tip off other drivers who have not yet acquired these valuable skills. Even tourists catch on sooner or later. When these techniques become too widely known, there is a lesser chance of success when applying them.

Taxicabs

When it comes to Boston Driving, nobody does it better than your typical neighborhood cab drivers. They can cut off without looking and blast through yellow and red lights with surgical precision. Cabbies' driving abilities should always be respected, but they can act extremely belligerent toward other drivers at times. Counter-harassment measures are often called for, but watch it: most cab

Your chariot awaits you at Harvard Square.

drivers carry a set of tire irons with them, and they're not always used for changing tires.

While the cab drivers themselves are very tough individuals, their vehicles certainly are not. Since cab companies collect no fares on an idle car, they naturally try to keep their fleets in service as close to twenty-four hours per day as possible. This means that when a cab comes in limping after a twelve-hour shift, there is only time enough for a quick first-aid job. In some of the larger garages, this treatment is usually applied by the company mechanic, who is well-trained in the art of bubble-gum-and-spit repair. After thirty years or 300,000 miles (whichever comes first), the cab is probably even less roadworthy than it looks. Most cabbies know that in the event of a collision their cars will more than likely crumble into a pile of rust chips. Seasoned Boston Drivers realize this and make the most of it.

In good traffic and in bad, taxi drivers love to tailgate. The alert Boston Driver can turn this weakness into an advantage and get a few laughs out of it besides. Cabbies tailgate because they are extremely impatient. If a cabbie ends up behind you in traffic, he will try to intimidate you into yielding. Don't even consider letting that happen; slow down and hold your lane. You could even try slowing down with the parking brakes, so your brake lights don't give you away. When the cabbie becomes irritated enough to try to pass you, he will change lanes, and you do the same. If you time it properly, he will still be behind you going 10 or 15 m.p.h. slower than he wants. When he tries to switch back, you switch back as well.

After playing this game for a while, the cabbie will get the message that you are deliberately harassing him. If you look in your rear-view mirror at this point, you may be able to see the steam rising from his collar. When he is finally able to accelerate by you, give him a big grin as he passes, and his blood pressure will climb right through the roof. You can then bask in the satisfaction of having beaten him at his own game.

Cab drivers do not always try to leave you behind in a cloud of dust, however. Cabbies have been known to go unbearably slowly when they are "cruising" for fares. Worse, if they spot a live customer, they will go to any length make a pick-up. This could include an abrupt stop, sudden lane changes, or even a U-turn into a convenient double-parking space. If one of these creatures crosses your path, give a couple of long blasts on your horn. It may not get them to move, but it will certainly make you feel better, and it may make them squirm a little bit.

In some of the heavier trafficked parts of town, taxi stands offer convenient illegal parking. By now you realize that a parking ticket is not what you should be worried about. To a cab driver, a taxi stand is holy ground. If you park in one for any length of time, you are likely to find out what those tire irons are really used for.

COMMANDMENT 10

Tread not in the pathway of a taxicab,
lest its driver wreak vengeance upon
thee with a tire iron.

Cadillacs

Wealthy, obnoxious, and invariably inept, Cadillac drivers view the world through the portals of their very own Sherman Tanks. By "Cadillac" we are referring to not only the traditional oversize models, but also the Lincoln Continental and any other cars in the general pimpmobile class. In the Boston area, where small cars have been in vogue since the Ted Williams era, Caddies make an even more obvious spectacle of themselves than they do elsewhere.

So even if you have no idea what a Cadillac looks like, you can easily spot one on the highway. Caddies love to get in the left lane

The finest and shiniest Detroit has to offer

and go 20 m.p.h. below the speed limit. If you should happen to pass one on the right, however, don't be surprised if the Cadillac driver suddenly and briefly snaps back to reality, accelerates to 80 m.p.h., and passes you back with a contemptuous sneer and a cloud of premium exhaust. Apparently, they consider it a personal affront to be passed by any car worth less than $35,000. They then slow back down to 40 m.p.h., as if the whole incident never happened. To understand the reason for this strange, but typical Cadillac behavior, you will simply have to go out and buy one yourself.

Occasionally you will see a Cadillac barreling down the highway at a constant speed of 75 m.p.h. or more. This indicates that the cruise control is engaged, and the driver is therefore busy mixing drinks while watching the news on the onboard Sony Trinitron. So if you should see the Tank in your rear-view mirror gaining on you, waste no time changing lanes, and you may live to make your next car insurance payment.

Cadillacs are easy to spot in the city as well. Although they are not generally too wide for a single lane, their drivers obviously think they are. On major city streets having four lanes, Cadillac drivers will require at least two of them. When they turn, they always cut short their left turns and make their right turns so wide that they have to start from the left lane. Even the worst MBTA bus drivers can execute neater turns than a Cadillac driver. And finally, when they are lucky enough to find street parking spaces big enough to suit their needs, Cadillac drivers demonstrate no conception whatsoever of parallel parking. Most of the time they simply drive forward into the space, leaving the rear end of the car sticking out into traffic.

Despite the physical advantages of Cadillacs and the obnoxious behavior of their drivers, the skilled Boston Driver will have little difficulty handling these dinosaurs of the road. While Cadillac drivers do like to execute intimidating maneuvers, they do it out of insecurity, just like a typical street bully. But at the slightest threat of a cutoff or sidesqueeze, they will yield, because they are deathly afraid of an accident. After all, it might scratch the paint, and that would be a severe blow to the Caddy owners ego. In the event of a showdown between a late model Cadillac and your 1992 Ford Escort, it is clear who has more to lose. After all, your Escort is not going to need $5,000 worth of body work after a collision; chances are, it won't look too different from before.

Because of their bulk and the cowardly nature of their drivers, Cadillacs are the easiest cars on the road to block. The only thing guaranteed not to work against a Cadillac is a large dose of your horn. Sitting in a mink-lined, gas-guzzling, environmentally controlled fortress, the driver is not likely to hear it.

Honda Civics

Honda Civics have evolved quite a bit over the last few years, but they've long been a favorite of an obnoxious class of Boston Drivers. "Civic" is a misnomer for these cars; they are constantly darting and poking and swirling in a most uncivic manner.

Civic owners think that the compactness and good maneuverability of their cars give them special license to manipulate traffic for their purposes. While the Cadillac owners philosophy is "I can do

Honda Civic: the durable Japanese Beetle

what I want because I'm bigger than you," the Civic owners attitude is "I can do what I want because you can't catch me." Favorite maneuvers are quick cutoffs and lane changes on both the highway and city streets. Civics' small wheelbase gives them exceptional ability to weave. They can make turns very rapidly around a small radius as well; this makes it fairly easy for them to do a U-turn across four lanes of traffic into an undersized parking space.

Because of the inherent quickness and maneuverability of the Civic, Boston Drivers must keep their basic skills sharper than ever when confronting one of these insects on wheels. The Civic's weakness is that, like the Cadillac, it cannot afford an accident. While the Caddy owner worries about chipping the paint, Civic owners worry about becoming blobs of chopped meat and tin foil. Civics have never been known for their durability, and their owners approach maintenance with a "drive till it drops" philosophy. All that protects the driver in the event of a front-end collision is some sheet-metal, air, and prayer.

Therefore, the best defense against a Civic is to make the driver think that its wings are about to be clipped. If one is weaving around you, close the "guillotine" (see Chapter IV, "Weaving"). Even if you are unable to actually prevent the car from getting through, you can still enjoy the satisfaction of making its driver sweat. If a Civic in an oncoming lane tries to sneak a left turn across your lane in front of you, show your savvy by rushing the intersection and making it close. As the Civic goes by, assault the driver with the longest and loudest blast your horn can muster. This may scare the people inside enough to make the driver think twice before attempting such a stunt again—especially in Boston.

Ultimately, Honda's Civic model will go the way of the $1.00 bleacher ticket. Honda has made recent Civics a little higher priced, more reliable, and boring, leaving the classic little sports model as the only truly maneuverable heir to the line. People who bought Civics because they were affordable are growing older, moving to the suburbs, and buying Camrys. Soon the Civic will disappear into the sunset like the Model T and the VW Beetle before it. For Boston Drivers, that day can't come soon enough.

Advanced Turns

In Chapter IV we discussed basic left turns and U-turns. These techniques should suffice for most common situations. After mastering the additional refinements described in this section, you will have the capability to turn anywhere, anytime, under any conditions.

Turn from the Wrong Lane

Even the most well-prepared Boston Drivers will occasionally face the problem of making a left turn from the right lane or a right turn from the left lane (or any turn from the center lane of a three-lane road). Most of the time, this situation arises because the driver is uncertain about which way to turn, or arrives at the desired intersection before expecting to do so. Without a working knowledge of techniques for wrong-lane turns, the helpless driver will needlessly waste precious time circling around in an attempt to correct the mistake. We must point out that the attempt is often futile since the street layout of the Boston area is such that retracing one's tracks takes at least forty-five minutes, if it is possible at all.

When you are confronted with the necessity of making a turn from the wrong lane, the simplest solution is to "slip in." This is accomplished by executing a routine cutoff or sidesqueeze to get into the proper lane, time permitting. If absolutely necessary, you could slow down to buy additional time. The slip-in maneuver should be applied when you are sure you are in the wrong lane and want to take corrective action.

On the other hand, if you are on a road with two lanes in each direction and you are approaching your turn unsure of whether you want to go left or right the best course of action is to execute a block by straddling the two lanes (see Chapter IV, "Blocking"). This should prevent any cars from trying to pass you, giving you the option of waiting until the last possible moment to make up your mind which way to turn.

If the road is three lanes in each direction, however, the situation is more complicated because traditional blocking alone will not do the job. We recommend the Guerrilla Blocking Tactic introduced to Boston by a noted Southeast Asian cab driver now living in Southie. When executing the Guerrilla Blocking Tactic, it is absolutely essential to weave so wildly that other drivers become convinced you are drunk. The effect is enhanced if the other drivers can see you clutching a can of beer as you lie slumped over the steering wheel. As you get closer to the intersection, block the two right lanes while signaling a left turn (or vice versa). If any drivers still had any notions of trying to squeeze by you up to this point, this open-field tactic should put an end to them.

Even if you run completely out of time and find yourself at the intersection still in the wrong lane, don't give up. If the light is red, and cars are stopped at the intersection, the problem becomes one of jockeying for position. At worst you can stay where you are, wait

The Guerrilla Blocking Tactic

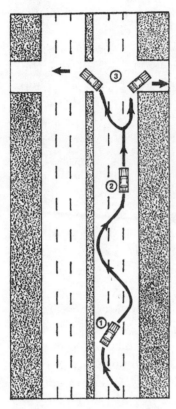

1. Weave wildly to scare off other drivers.
2. Block two lanes near intersection.
3. Make your move left or right.

for the green light, and proceed into the intersection.

Another, more elegant method that almost always works is the "standing cutoff." This maneuver is executed by inching the front of your car ahead of another vehicle stopped in the adjacent lane. Once you have established position, you have done the hard part. The cars behind you in both directions are now blocked. When the light changes to green and traffic ahead of you begins to move, simply complete the cutoff of the car you have already nosed out; you will seldom encounter any real resistance. Be professional and businesslike about it. There is no need to look back and gloat over the frustration written all over the face of your victim.

Oncoming Traffic Left Turns

In most cities, executing a left turn can be one of the most time-consuming and frustrating of all driving exercises. However, in Boston, decades of research have produced several innovative procedures for dealing with this problem. One of the best is referred to as the Oncoming Traffic Left Turn.

The essence of the Oncoming Traffic Left Turn is not that it is made from the *wrong* lane, but that it is made from the *oncoming*

The Standing Cutoff

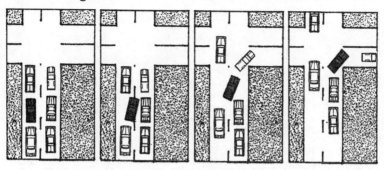

1. Start.

2. Establish position in other lane; wait for green light.

3. When space permits, pull completely into other lane.

4. Finish turn from proper lane.

lane—on the other side of the double line. This technique is applicable when you are in line for a left turn, but stymied because the lead driver doesn't have what it takes to cut across the traffic and finish off the left turn. No doubt he or she is an out-of-state Cadillac driver who is visiting Boston for the first time. When confronting this situation, you must pull into the oncoming lane, rush the intersection, and cut off the lead car to complete your left turn. Naturally, this maneuver is risky since any oncoming traffic that slips through the intersection could place you in an embarrassing position with no possible escape. Therefore, the maneuver should be executed as quickly as possible. The best time to move is when the lead car finally begins its own left turn, thereby blocking the oncoming lanes.

Properly applied, the Oncoming Lane Left Turn can save the alert Boston Driver a great deal of time. In addition to the situation described above, this maneuver may be used any time the first car in line fails to move, whatever the reason. For example, the lead car could be stalled or broken down. More likely, the confused turkey

The Oncoming Lane Left Turn

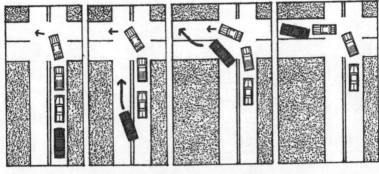

1. Start.

2. Pull into oncoming lane.

3. Rush intersection; cut off lead car.

4. Finish.

driving the lead car will suddenly decide he or she doesn't really want to turn left after all but can't go straight from a left-turn-only lane, or perhaps has let the intersection clog with traffic. So everybody sits there—until you make your move into the oncoming lane. One final situation where you should consider using this maneuver is whenever you see two fourteen-year-old boys get out and run away from a shiny new sports car. If they leave the doors open and the motor running, and you can hear police sirens in the distance, it's a good bet that car is going nowhere fast.

Gas Station Turns

In Chapter IV we discussed how valuable gas stations can be in assisting the Boston Driver in making U-turns. This is only one of dozens of possible uses of gas stations in advanced Boston Driving. (Where no gas station is available, vacant lots and small shopping centers may be used instead.) This section will demonstrate that there are certainly many other uses for gas stations besides filling up your tank.

Basic Gas Station Right Turn

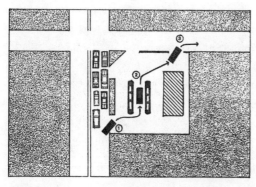

1. Turn into gas station.
2. Pause at pumps.
3. Continue to opposite exit and turn.

Right Turns

This is the simplest of the gas station maneuvers, recommended for Boston Drivers who are trying these techniques for the first time. It is most commonly used to avoid waiting in a long line of traffic to take a right turn. When proceeding more slowly than you'd like toward the intersection, simply pull into a convenient corner gas station. Pass by the pumps and pretend to look disgusted at the prices; this gives you the excuse you need to continue to the opposite driveway, from which you can turn onto the cross street. Of course, you didn't really need gas right then anyway; the whole purpose of this act is to legitimize your detour through the station. While there is some question as to whether this maneuver is legal or not, it has become a standard Boston Driving procedure. It is also the basic element of the more complex gas station maneuvers to be described in subsequent paragraphs.

Oncoming Traffic/Gas Station Left Turn Combination

When executing an oncoming lane left turn, always give a quick glance to the left to see whether there is a gas station on the near corner. If so, you can complete your turn faster and easier with less risk. You begin this maneuver in the usual way by pulling into the oncoming traffic lane. Proceed into the gas station up to the pumps. As before, change your mind" about getting gas and drive to the opposite entrance to the station. Make a simple left turn or a Boston Left Turn onto the cross street, and you can chalk up another several minutes saved through expert technique. Leave all the worries of red and green lights and nasty opposing traffic to all those cars that were formerly ahead of you and are still waiting to get through.

Straight-Ahead-on-Red

The introduction of right-turn-on-red has opened the doors for many innovations in urban driving techniques. In Massachusetts this has been carried a step further: expert Boston Drivers are now successfully engineering straight-ahead-on-red maneuvers (without incurring any unwanted moving violations, of course). The straight-ahead-on-red maneuver is a combination of a simple gas station right turn and basic left and right turn. Essentially, all that is involved is to turn into the gas station (and decide you don't need gas), proceed to the opposite driveway, make a left onto the cross street (which has a green light) and a right onto your original street This is ideal for intersections with long light cycles, at times when you see the light change to red as you arrive. If the light should change back to green before you complete the right turn onto your original street, you will be facing a red light on the cross street. This may present a problem if heavy traffic from your original direction makes it more difficult for you to pull off a right-turn-on-red. However, this is an excellent opportunity to brush up on your cut-off and sidesqueeze techniques. You may also be lucky enough to find another friendly gas station through which to turn right.

If the left turn out of the gas station is blocked by a median or by dense traffic, you will instead have to make a right turn out of the station, followed by a U-turn, to achieve the same effect. This, of course, takes more time and therefore presents a greater risk of missing the light. However, there are dozens of intersections

The Straight-Ahead-on-Red Maneuver

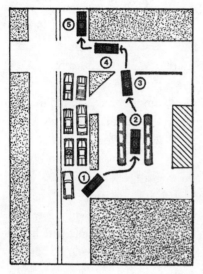

1. Turn left into gas station.
2. Pause at pumps.
3. Proceed to opposite exit.
4. Turn left onto cross street.
5. Turn right onto original street.

throughout the Greater Boston area whose light cycles are so long that any drunk driver could effortlessly execute these turns five times within a single cycle, and many do so just for fun.

Left-Turn-on-Red

A variation on the straight-ahead-on-red maneuver described above can be used to execute left turns on red as well. The only caveat is that the turn must be started from the right lane (i.e., the wrong lane). It is performed by executing a straight-ahead-on-red maneuver, but omitting the final right turn so as to proceed directly through the intersection on the cross street.

Sidewalk Driving and Sidewalk Parking

Many drivers, even some good-to-excellent Boston Drivers, suffer from the misconception that sidewalks are off-limits to them.

However, sidewalks are no less a part of the skilled Boston Driver's equipment than the steering wheel. After all, pedestrians walk on your streets, why shouldn't you drive on their sidewalks?

There are a surprising number of situations where it can be quite advantageous to go up on the sidewalk. For example, a sidewalk can be used in place of a gas station or empty lot to pass a slow car ahead of you. Simply roll up over the curb, accelerate forward while on the sidewalk (carefully avoiding trees, parking meters, pedestrians, and assorted other hazards), and squeeze back into the traffic stream when convenient. Sidewalks can also be used to skirt around construction sites, loading and unloading trucks, and block parties. A final situation where you might need a sidewalk is when you are going down a one-way street the wrong way. If another car should have the audacity to come down the street the right way, you might have to pull onto the sidewalk to let it by. An incidental benefit of this approach is that once you are on the sidewalk, you are no longer going the wrong way, since sidewalk traffic is always permitted in both directions.

On crowded city streets, every last bit of space must be considered for its parking potential, and this certainly includes sidewalks. Consider the advantages: they bring you directly to your doorstep, and there is never a meter. They are a convenient last resort when no other parking is available. On narrow, one-lane roads (e.g., Beacon Hill) where there is not enough room to park in the street without obstructing traffic, sidewalk parking is the answer. In doing so, you run much less risk of falling into the jaws of the not-so-friendly neighborhood tow truck. Furthermore, you don't have to worry about moving your car on street cleaning days since you aren't on the street anymore.

In the winter, when the snow prevents you from seeing where the street ends and the sidewalk begins, you may consider them to be one and the same for parking purposes. This is necessary because the snow takes up so much of the available parking (and driving) area; therefore, you can park anywhere with impunity.

One final note on sidewalks: they are excellent for avoiding Big Dig construction delays. Some of them even have lane markers for guiding rush-hour traffic.

Deceptive Use of Signals

Every car comes equipped with a number of built-in signaling devices, including directional signals, a horn, high-beam headlights, and flashers. However, few drivers know how to make optimum use of this equipment in achieving their Boston Driving goals. These tools are at your fingertips whenever you are behind the wheel; don't overlook their potential for expediting your trip, as well as for harassing your fellow Boston Drivers.

Directionals

Besides their normal use of notifying other drivers of your intention to make a left or right turn, directionals have several other uses as well. Actually, most drivers misuse their directionals by signaling too early. It is best not to signal until the middle of the turn; that way, your legal obligation to signal has been fulfilled, but no one else has time to react.

Your directionals can also be used in the situation where you want to harass and ultimately shake off a tailgater. When being followed too closely for comfort, signal a lane change and then gradually decelerate without actually changing lanes. At first the tailgater will be reluctant to pass you, since he or she will think you are about to switch lanes yourself, and will have to slow down. By the time you are down to about 10 m.p.h., he or she will get the message, pass you, and be out of your life forever.

Another possible opportunity occurs when you are in an unfamiliar part of town looking for a particular street to turn into. As you approach each intersection, you signal a turn (it doesn't really matter whether you signal left or right). If the intersection contains the street you are looking for, you turn and end the matter.

Otherwise, you continue on straight, leaving your confused fellow drivers to guess at your real intentions. Since they don't know when you are going to turn, or which way, or even whether you're going to turn at all, they are likely to give you the run of the road. This is especially effective when combined with the Guerrilla Blocking Tactic described earlier in this chapter.

A final use of the directional is to announce that you have completed a cutoff. Just as you are pulling in front of your victim, signal briefly just to let him or her know you're there. Of course, the other driver knew that already, so your signal is just a way of rubbing it in. This is the Boston Driving equivalent of the Red Auerbach victory cigar.

Horn

Horns were originally intended to give the driver a means to warn other drivers or pedestrians of a potentially hazardous situation. However, in routine Boston Driving, horns are never used for this purpose. As the reader is surely aware by now, warning other drivers of one's intentions is the road to Boston Driving ruin. In the current environment, horns are used strictly for recreation, intimidation, and harassment.

The most basic use of a horn is to persuade drivers in front of you at an intersection to get moving after a light turns green. One second is the maximum amount of reaction time you should tolerate before blasting away. While the leading drivers may not be able to go right away because of cross-traffic running the red light, this is their problem, not yours. After all, you have better things to do with your time than to spend all day stuck at a green light. If you have ever been the lead car under such circumstances, you know how intense the pressure of hundreds of horns honking behind you can be, especially when there is no clear path in front of you.

Another common use of the horn is to deter another driver from executing a cutoff against you. The experienced Boston Driver should be aware of and on the lookout for the telltale signs of a cut-off, so that he or she can honk some sense into the opposing driver. These include edging slowly toward your lane, passing you, looking directly at you or your car, and (strictly for novices) signaling. Your blast of horn must authoritatively convey the message that (1) you are not going to let anyone in front of you, and (2) everyone else should revise their driving plans accordingly. You must time your blast properly, for if you are late, you will have already been cut off. In this case your horn will do no more than call attention to other drivers that you have been whipped.

You should take advantage of every opportunity to honk your horn to intimidate pedestrians as well. They don't even have to be in the street: if one threatens to step off the curb toward your path, you should immediately speed up and give a long, loud blast. If you execute quickly and effectively, your pedestrian victim will most likely beat a hasty retreat back onto the sidewalk. Acting drunk or out of control will increase your chances of success.

Finally, Boston Drivers have traditionally used their horns to commemorate happy occasions. For example, horn concerts can be heard in Kenmore Square after every Red Sox win. They are also used to celebrate New Year's Eve, Friday afternoon at 5:00, and any other event worth noting. For some reason, these horn-honking celebrations always seem to occur at times when traffic is jammed, and no one has anything better to do. Rumor has it that this practice will cease when the Red Sox win their next World Series; it has been going on since they won their last one in 1918.

Flashers

If you followed the car-shopping advice in Chapter I, you might have actually found a car that does not have flashers. (By "flashers" we are referring to parking lights blinking in unison, not dirty old men in trench coats.) However, they have been standard equipment since the 1960s, so virtually every car will be equipped with them. In effect, flashers are a visible horn; they are intended to signal that the driver is doing something unusual or is in trouble. In the world of Boston Driving, however, everyone else is in trouble if your flashers are on. They convey the intimidating message that you are executing an offensive driving maneuver, and other drivers had best stay clear.

Flashers might be used if you are going much faster or slower than other traffic. When you are on the highway going 20 m.p.h. faster than the traffic stream, flashers make weaving considerably easier. When driving slowly, you can use flashers to facilitate cruising for parking or to enhance the Guerrilla Blocking Tactic (see discussion under "Turn from Wrong Lane"). In the latter case, flashers signal a left and a right turn simultaneously, so you're covered, regardless of which way you decide to turn.

One final use of flashers is in manufacturing a parking space where absolutely no other is available. The combination of a raised hood and flashers guarantees thirty minutes of free parking anywhere in the city, including the Governor's space under the State House.

High Beams

High-beam headlights can be used not only for lighting up the roadway on a dark night but also as an offensive driving tool. Most drivers will do almost anything to avoid the stinging, blinding glare of these lights, even if it requires them to slow down or yield. It is a common practice to blink your high beams at oncoming drivers who may inadvertently have their own high beams on and aimed at you. If they do not immediately switch to low beams, you can leave your high beams on so as to do unto others as they have done unto you. Most drivers get the message sooner or later, however.

High beams can also work wonders in clearing the left lane of slow-moving traffic, especially Cadillacs. Tailgate as closely as possible before lighting up the entire car with your high beams. Your victims will hopefully get the impression that you are giving them the third degree. Because of the blinding glare, they can't see you, but you can see them perfectly well. Few drivers can withstand more than a few seconds of such intimidation before yielding. If you flash your lights on and off, they might even think you're the police and pull over, expecting the worst. Once your lane is clear, leave your high beams on to light up the roadway in front of you. In effect, you have "claimed" that road space for your own personal use. Anyone who would then wander into it would do so at their own risk.

All of the Above

The simultaneous use of high beams, horn, and flashers looks and sounds like an emergency. Nothing instills fear into the hearts of drivers quite like the sight of a car barreling toward them with high beams and flashers on, horn blaring, and a madman behind the wheel. They will usually get out of your way as fast as they can. This technique is especially useful for traveling at top speed down the "middle lane" of the Callahan Tunnel when you have only ten minutes to catch a 5:30 P.M. flight out of Logan Airport. You might also try this if you are mired in Kenmore Square after an extra-inning ballgame and are late for an important dinner appointment. It stands to reason that this maneuver should be applied sparingly, lest its impact be diluted from overuse. Short of installing a police siren and a bubble gum machine on top of your car, this is the most potent medicine available to Boston Drivers. It will enable you to cut through the worst traffic jams like a hot knife through butter.

Hand Signals

During driver training, you were probably taught to use hand signals as an alternative to directionals to tell other drivers where you are going. However, in the Boston area, hand signals are used to tell other drivers where to go. Unlike on the football field, Boston Drivers are never called for "illegal use of the hands." Hand signals may not get you ahead of opposing drivers, but they are a widely used harassment technique. While the extended middle finger remains the most popular hand signal, there are literally hundreds of other forms, with new ones being invented every day. This is one reason why most Boston Drivers prefer the summer months: with the windows routinely open, they can extend their hands on a moment's notice. The practice of giving hand signals is so popular that many stores now sell phosphorescent gloves for night signaling. Further research on the subject will undoubtedly produce many techniques for communicating with hand signals in the years to come.

9

The Future of Boston Driving

Since its founding in 1630, Boston has always been a dynamic city, constantly adapting to new times. Dredging the harbor, creating Back Bay out of landfill, and leveling the forgettable Scollay Square to build Government Center were all major Boston reinventions. The Big Dig, as the largest public works project since the Egyptian pyramids, is the most recent transforming initiative. But it will certainly not be the last. As Boston evolves in the coming century, Boston Drivers will change with the times as well.

The future will be exciting and maybe a bit scary, with much promise. But some things won't change—there will still be intermittent periods of snow, ice, and gridlock to look forward to. Tourists will remain the scourge of Boston streets, and you'll still be able to take advantage of their hopeless driving skills.

With some help from the crystal ball we won at Revere Beach, we would like to present a futuristic look of what's in store for Boston Drivers for the rest of this century. We can absolutely guarantee that these forecasts will be accurate, knowing that this book will be out of print long before anyone could find us and hold us accountable for them.

Dateline—April 2020. Boston's rush hour is now a continuous event, extending from 5:00 A.M. to 1:00 A.M. No daylight hours (and few nighttime hours) are safe from the continuous onslaught of gridlock traffic. Furthermore, with the city doing well and continuing to grow nicely over the past generation, the overnight parking situation in the urban residential areas has now become desperate. Garage parking downtown now costs more than $5,000 per month. Many of Boston's financial services outfits now sell "parking garage annuities," where, for the modest sum of the GNP of a small country, you can buy parking space rights extending up to thirty years in the future. Parking space rights have become the latest trendy real estate investment.

Boston Drivers have coped with the parking shortage in a number of clever ways, the most popular of which is to rent out their parking space(s) for a tidy sum when they (and their cars) will be out of town. The going rate for renting a space for the weekend is roughly equivalent in cost to a week-long vacation for two in Aruba. The *Forbes* billionaires list now has several Boston residents who were savvy enough to cash in on the great parking space boom of the past decade.

When you can get moving, toll payments on the major bridges and tunnels are now completely automatic and cashless. Fast Lane tags are universal: cars pass by the sensor and the money is taken from the account, just like an ATM. If the account is empty or the car is not known to the system, then a 250-pound wrecking ball falls out of the sky and is precisely guided to land on the car's front hood. This has tended to encourage drivers to keep their toll accounts in good standing.

These toll payments have been a boon to Boston's finances, as well as those of many of the surrounding communities. Using this same electronic tag system, tolls are charged for street parking and for driving through particular intersections. Some innovative towns have instituted charges for each minute spent driving on their streets. With Boston's streets approaching gridlock, many people have been forced to declare personal bankruptcy before they get home.

The good news is that this high-tech approach to vehicle sur-veillance has eliminated car theft. Boston's last known professional car thief was caught in 2017, when the toll sensor in the stolen car ran out of money. He was convicted and sentenced to ten hours of watching replays of Bill Buckner's World Series highlights. The harsh sentence no doubt convinced many other copycat criminals that there are better ways to make a living.

Dateline—June 2050. The opening of the Gloucester-to-Quincy causeway marked the completion of the "Bigger Dig" project, whose goal was to fill in the entire Boston Bay. This made the Route 128/I-95 combination a continuous circular loop around the city. Confusion reigned among many Boston Drivers, who, if they went north far enough on the loop highway, would end up south. Many drivers were forced to accept the notion that their world is round.

All the new land available for growth made Boston the fastest-growing American city. Logan Airport was relocated about 5 miles farther east, and new towns sprang up in between. In keeping with tradition, the new town of Dukakis (named for a prominent twen-tieth-century governor and presidential candidate) passed a law pro-hibiting the posting of readable street signs in the town. Lots of peo-ple got lost trying to navigate through Dukakis, but that was chalked up to being part of the Boston Driving experience.

Most urban traffic is now controlled by computers, with traffic lights set according to the number of cars traveling in each direc-tion. This has increased the average speed driving through the city to 12 m.p.h. A recent story in the *Boston Globe* marveled at the progress, noting that the average speed through Boston's streets in 1900 was 11 m.p.h. with horses and buggies. The article expressed optimism that in the next 150 years the average speed might increase to as much as 13 m.p.h. Now that's real progress.

Dateline—October 2095. Technical advances have taken all the stress out of urban transportation. Cars now have the ability to trav-el airborne, which made it possible for traffic to be stacked up in vertical lanes beginning in the 2070s. At first this led to some creativity—every driver had the option to cut off the opposition either horizontally or vertically. However, passing your fellow driver underneath *and* upside down was discouraged because it often deposited auto and body parts on the surrounding terrain, requiring a costly cleanup that further took away from the city's snow removal budget.

The last quarter of the twenty-first century has seen great progress in improving traffic flow. Not only are traffic lights and lanes run by computer, but also a robotic driver with speed-of-light reflexes controls each individual car. It is not at all uncommon to be zipping between crowded downtown buildings at 75 m.p.h., all the while sipping some coffee and watching CNN. Nobody has to execute a Cutoff or Boston Left Turn maneuver anymore, because the computers keep everyone away from each other. There are no traffic lights to worry about, and every other car's robotic driver is the same idiot that's driving yours.

Furthermore, since traffic can be stacked vertically, high above the city, there is no longer any need for bridges or tunnels. The nearly 100-year-old underground Central Artery (the centerpiece of the Big Dig project of 1991–2005) became obsolete and was recently converted to a pedestrian shopping mall.

The species we used to know as Boston Drivers is all but extinct, and Boston Driving is becoming, to some extent, a lost art. To be sure, there are groups of hobbyists that have cars with their robot drivers disabled, who gather in abandoned roadways and actually operate the cars *manually* (how crude). These cars have *hand and foot controls* that are used for maneuvering. They also sometimes have to *stop to let each other pass by*, or else risk a *deadly collision*.

Admittedly, it does take some skill to operate these dinosaur cars. As a result, Boston Driving has been added as an event in the next Olympic Games. There was some debate as to whether Boston Driving was a summer or winter sport. In the end it was decided that summer and winter driving were two different skills, so it was added to both. Trained Boston Drivers are expected to have a lock on the gold medal for a long time to come.

Coincidentally, the year 2095 is the 200th anniversary of the birth of Babe Ruth and the 100th anniversary of the opening of the Ted Williams Tunnel, the first usable product of the Big Dig. Therefore, it is altogether fitting that 2095 is also the year the Red Sox defeated the Chicago Cubs 4 games to 0 to win their first World Series since 1918. The key factor was Boston's mayor organizing an expedition to go to Babe Ruth's grave and publicly apologize to him for the shabby treatment he endured while in Boston. With the legendary "Curse of the Bambino" lifted, the Sox cruised to an easy victory. While Bostonians around the globe celebrated, other big city mayors conducted their own graveside apologies to their dead sports heroes in an attempt to level the playing field. We'll have to "wait till next year" to find out who else's apologies were accepted.

Final Exam

Test your Boston Driving knowledge by taking this twenty-four-question, multiple-choice examination. It might highlight some weak spots in your training that you should brush up on. Answers and scoring instructions may be found following the test.

1. You are trying to pull out of a parking space, but your car does not move. You hear a whirring sound outside your car window. This indicates:

    A. your dentist has opened an outdoor office.

    B. boating season is here.

    C. it's wintertime in Boston.

    D. it's garbage pickup day.

2. Filene's is having a once-in-a-lifetime lingerie sale on the Saturday before Christmas. You arrive on the scene five minutes before closing and can't find a legitimate parking space. What should you do?

    A. Double-park, raise your hood, put your flashers on, and run inside.

    B. Try to bribe the nearest Girl Scout on the sidewalk to pick up some choice items for you.

    C. Give up and go home.

    D. Drive through the main entrance, take a right at the second cash register, and follow to the lingerie department.

3. Boston streets were the result of:

   A. the volcanic eruption of Mt. Bunker in 250 B.C.

   B. seventeenth-century cow paths.

   C. an early resident's love of spaghetti.

   D. a conscientious and comprehensive urban plan.

4. Which of the following is the best car for Boston Driving?

   A. a brand new Infiniti, with the sticker still on it.

   B. a 1982 Chevette with 180,000 miles on it, no hubcaps, a burned out muffler, and lots of rust.

   C. a 2002 Porsche 911.

   D. a late model Sherman Tank, fully equipped with howitzers and machine guns.

5. A Sidesqueeze is:

   A. a method for merging into dense streams of traffic.

   B. a sandwich served at Bertucci's.

   C. a way to go between two parked cars.

   D. a nice thing to happen on a date.

6. The Boston Police pull you over for driving the wrong way down Berkeley Street at rush hour. What is the most likely outcome?

   A. They will charge you with drunk driving, arrest you, and impound your car.

   B. They will issue you a ticket for driving the wrong way down a one-way street.

   C. They will give you a warning for having a broken taillight.

   D. They will ask you what you think of the Bruins' chances this year.

7. Back Street is a good place to go to:

   A. park in a tow zone.

   B. travel rapidly through Back Bay.

   C. avoid snowdrifts.

   D. get mugged.

8. You receive a $40 ticket for parking in a tow zone. You should:

   A. pay it and be thankful you weren't towed.

   B. pay $20 and hope they take it.

   C. take the case to the Supreme Court.

   D. leave it on your windshield and park in the same place the next day.

9. The chains carried in the trunk of most taxicabs are:

   A. deadly weapons to ensure traffic justice.

   B. only used during the winter.

   C. good for towing other cars or stubborn passengers.

   D. a gift for the cabbie's girlfriend.

10. The "Beat-the-Green" technique is:

   A. a recipe for making pureed vegetables.

   B. a way to go straight ahead on red.

   C. a quick left turning technique.

   D. rarely successful against the Celtics.

11. In the Callahan and Sumner tunnels there is an abundance of:

   A. dirt.

   B. fresh air.

   C. happy motorists.

   D. parking spaces.

12. Behind you is a car with high beams and flashers on and horn blaring. The man driving looks like a wide-eyed lunatic. You surmise that:

   A. he is a police officer in an unmarked car.

   B. he is annoyed because he can't turn off his high beams, horn, and flashers.

   C. he is desperately seeking a public restroom.

   D. his radio is on so loud that he doesn't notice.

13. Cutoffs are:

    A. never attempted by Cadillac drivers.
    B. done to get ahead of opposing drivers.
    C. the best things to wear to the Esplanade in the summer.
    D. impossible on Storrow Drive.

14. Beacon Hill has great quantities of:

    A. wide, navigable streets.
    B. smooth, well-surfaced roads.
    C. free parking for visitors.
    D. none of the above.

15. You should never fix a fender-bender right away because:

    A. your insurance rates will go up.
    B. you have up to eleven months until the next inspection anyway.
    C. dents scare off other drivers.
    D. if you do, next week you will get hit in the same spot.

16. For a Boston Driver, the best use of a cellular phone is:

    A. to report accidents to the police.
    B. to call radio talk shows and complain about the deplorable conditions of roads and highways in the city.
    C. to tell your spouse you're tied up in traffic and will be home in just two hours.
    D. to use someone else's antenna to mix drinks at a tailgate party.

17. F.L.T. stands for:

    A. Frequent Left Turner.
    B. Fast Lane Tagholder.
    C. Fairly Light Traffic.
    D. Focaccia, Lettuce, & Tomato.

18. During the winter you find a lonely parking space dug out of the snow, with a trash can in its center. This means that:

    A. garbage will be collected the next morning.
    B. there is a fire hydrant underneath the trash can.
    C. you shouldn't park there unless you want your tires slashed.
    D. the neighborhood stray dog will get its supper tonight

19. A flashing green light signals that:

    A. the traffic signal is out of order.
    B. you should proceed ahead at double speed.
    C. swarms of pedestrians are nearby.
    D. the Celtics are playing at home tonight.

20. The most dangerous and foul-smelling hazard of Boston is:

    A. an Allston cab driver after a 12-hour shift.
    B. a barge of harbor sludge.
    C. a long-distance trucker who has jammed his rig in a Storrow Drive underpass.
    D. the Patriots locker room after an overtime loss.

21. To make up for the loss of parking spaces that had been under the old Central Artery, the city will:

    A. double the size of the Boston Common parking garage.
    B. issue new resident parking stickers in Dorchester.
    C. legalize sidewalk parking.
    D. none of the above.

22. You run into an endless back-up on the Tobin Bridge during afternoon rush hour. What mantra should you repeat to calm yourself down?

    A. "Make it in Massachusetts."
    B. "In another fifteen years, I can retire."
    C. "In a hundred years, what difference will it make?"
    D. "If you lived here, you'd be home now."

23. The land the Central Artery used to occupy will most likely:

    A. once again become part of Chinatown.
    B. be turned into a grassy public park.
    C. be preserved as a natural refuge for Boston's rats.
    D. provide housing for scores of disadvantaged law firms.

24. This test is harder than:

    A. a U-turn on Storrow Drive.
    B. hailing a cab in Roxbury.
    C. finding a street sign when you need one.
    D. passing the Massachusetts Learner's Permit exam.

Extra Credit

The Leonard P. Zakim Bunker Hill Bridge:

    A. connects Boston with Charlestown on I-93.
    B. contains 7 million feet of cable wire.
    C. resembles a harp on steroids.
    D. all of the above.

Answers

1. C	10. C	19. C
2. A	11. A	20. C
3. B	12. C	21. D
4. B	13. B	22. D
5. A	14. D	23. B
6. C	15. C	24. D
7. D	16. B	Extra Credit: D
8. D	17. B	
9. A	18. C	

Scoring

0-7 correct:	Hopeless Tourist
8–14 correct:	Suburban Weekender
15–20 correct:	City Commuter
21–24 correct:	Allston Cab Driver
more than 24 correct:	Compulsive Liar

About the Authors

Ira Gershkoff showed his aptitude for Boston Driving at a very early age, when he developed the habit of crossing the street, then looking both ways. A native of Haverhill, Massachusetts, Mr. Gershkoff's Boston Driving career began at an early age, when he drove himself and a friend to a Bruins' game at the Boston Garden, got lost on the way home, and ran out of gas. From that auspicious beginning, his career blossomed to the point that he set a single season record by collecting 1,272 unpaid parking tickets without a single moving violation. Mr. Gershkoff now works as consultant for the Federal Aviation Administration, doing research on the application of Boston Driving techniques to air traffic control.

While growing up in New York City, Richard Trachtman gave himself an early taste of Boston Driving experience by engineering catastrophic collisions on his H-O scale road-racing set. However, Mr. Trachtman began Boston Driving in earnest when he enrolled at M.I.T. and moved to the Boston area. Within a few months he had abandoned a promising career in astrophysics to sign on as a night driver for the Boston Cab Company. In the years that followed, he logged nearly half a million miles carrying everything from drunken sailors bound for the Combat Zone to urine samples bound for the laboratories of Beth Israel Hospital. Mr. Trachtman now works in Washington, D.C., as a full-time lobbyist dedicated to promoting legislation that would prohibit the sale, manufacture, and installation of "No Turn on Red" signs.